Dedication

To my wife, my partners and my friends

THE NECESSARY MONUMENT

Theo Crosby

Studio Vista London

© Theo Crosby 1970
Published in Great Britain by Studio Vista Limited
Blue Star House, Highgate Hill, London N19
Set in 9/11 Univers 689
Printed in Great Britain by Fletcher and Son Ltd, Norwich
Bound by Richard Clay Ltd, Bungay, Suffolk

SBN 289 79765 9 (paper)
    289 79775 6 (hardback)

Contents

Above and below: memorial plaque
on the southern approach of Tower
Bridge

Preface

Most members of my generation were weaned on the 'modern movement' and the past was interpreted for us by a generation of critics (Roger Fry, Sigfried Giedion, Nikolaus Pevsner, J. M. Richards), as a sometimes wayward but always inevitable preparation for our own revolutionary era. In effect, history was used highly selectively to justify the present and to promote a whole series of attitudes which seemed essential and inevitable.

The 'movement' was born in the early years of the century, at the moment when it became apparent that technology was entering a new phase: mass production. The possibilities of this new world of motor vehicles and flight, of radio and electric light were seen to be enormous, and marvellously liberating. In the arts, however, the problems of mass production had been a constant threat through most of the nineteenth century. Artists had welcomed and pioneered photography and within sixty years had seen their main source of income (the creation and control of images) disappear. From being a central, primary factor in society, the artist became a bohemian, a worker at the fringe.

This same process is now undermining the profession of the architect. Industrialization of building has come late to full mechanization, but the process will as surely make the concept of the architect as a form giver obsolete.

It has been pointed out that to achieve the maximum benefits of technology there has to be a continuous adaptation by society to the requirements of the technology. In particular, the intellectual and creative elements in society must be bent to the service of the machine. And to serve well, they must learn to love it.

This subservience has been so gradual and is now so complete as to be almost unconscious. The interdependence of the industrial state and the intellectual community has effects far outside the simple matter of providing technicians for the corporations, or grants for the study of potentially useful weaponry. It reaches into every minute part of our lives, altering our modes of perception and conditioning our understanding. Thus we learn to love frozen peas, because ordinary peas are quite simply not there. The taste of the natural vegetable is the merest memory. On the other hand we have a wide choice of equally frozen alternatives.

The same accommodation has been reached in the environmental sense. It is convenient for our miserably inept building industry to cover large areas with repetitive blocks of identical dwellings; at the same time this dehumanizing environment is accepted as socially good, because the system produces the maximum number of minimum homes for the least apparent cost. It has been, and is, accepted as inevitable.

Above: a Victorian building in the City of London which manages to retain a civilized scale and architectural complexity in the midst of barbarian redevelopment

In such a world, the past is an embarrassment. Old buildings are therefore considered pretentious and over decorated. It is no accident that the plainest style, the neo-classic or Georgian, has been the most esteemed for sixty years. Buildings with more content, the Baroque or late Victorian, have few friends.

Yet it is precisely this embarrassment that we should now begin to probe and understand, and to resolve, because it provides a key to our relation to the past and to the present. It may show a possible way out of our own impasse in relation to the machine. In our cities the monuments of the nineteenth century provide an abrasive element which our culture has as yet been unable to assimilate. Above all, they are enormous *examples* of an alternative mode of perception, of another set of priorities, an alternative to our accommodation to the industrial system.

The effect of this intellectual accommodation and acquiescence is now very obvious all around us. Cities once beautiful are now accepted as 'spoiled', and no-one quite knows why, though they tend to blame the planners.

One may as well blame the police for crime.

The necessary monument

The image of a city is made up of its landmarks, its monuments, and this book is an attempt to evaluate the role of the 'spectacular' building in several ways. In particular, there is the question of how far the purely economic role of a building can, or should be, subsumed by its other life as a spectacle; and also what is to be done with it when its primary function has been completed, and it has to subsist on its secondary roles.

This latter is a condition now affecting most of the great, apparently functional, buildings of the nineteenth century. Because of their commercial origins, they are subject to economic pressures and changes of use, which work against the automatic preservation accorded to more ancient monuments. Our society is as yet unwilling to support them entirely for their visual qualities, and at the same time cannot bring itself to allow them to be unceremoniously replaced.

The purely economic argument has the merits of simplicity: a building represents a certain capital outlay, from which a return can be expected for a specific period, as with any other investment. After the period has elapsed, the value has been earned and theoretically it would be logical and profitable to replace it with a new building, which would in turn be treated in the same way. Our cities would therefore go through continuous cycles of rebuilding, at progressively shorter intervals as our capital formation capacity grows with our technology.

There are, in fact, many areas of the world where this elementary system is in operation, but when looked at closely, it is not really very simple at all. Firstly, those cities which have a rapid renewal rate are always very new, pioneering settlements such as Sydney, Johannesburg or Los Angeles, caught in a vast population growth and a simultaneous increase in productivity. Their rapid turnover is due mainly to rising site values. If the land becomes more valuable than the buildings on it, a change becomes an economic necessity.

In societies where economic factors are allowed full play (once again in newly established, pioneering societies), the problem of the necessary but unwanted building does not arise, and in any case there are, by the very nature of the place, few such buildings.

In the maturely grown city, with a vast accumulation of structures, however, the problem is quite different, and the economics, like everything else, are no longer simple. A vast number of complicating factors have arisen, owing to the human activity in the years since the building was built; a million individual decisions have affected the building, the site and the neighbourhood. Values have

The necessary monument

risen or dropped, and above all, the community itself has become involved in decisions once left to the individual developer.

In the past twenty years the planner, as the agent of community involvement, has appeared on the scene, full of theories, in their own way often as simplistic as those of the nineteenth-century economists. His intervention in the environment has been almost uniformly deadening. Our surroundings are today in many respects infinitely worse than those of 150 years ago. Compared to the complex social and economic mechanisms of Nash's Regent's Park in London, a new town is as elementary as a box of children's blocks, and about as satisfactory to live in.

Yet our lives are infinitely more complicated than in 1820. Distance and time hold few terrors for us. We move easily all over the world, know a great deal of all cultures living and dead. Above all, there are so many more of us, all communicating as hard as we can. Our culture is a labyrinth, a vast storehouse of treasures instantly available; yet we live in miserable little boxes and in a growing squalor.

A fantastic contradiction.

We need to begin to look for a theory (for a theory is always necessary and without one no decision can ever be justified), which will allow us to build the correct environment without shame or guilt. This theory will have to accommodate a whole string of apparently contradictory factors, economic, social and political; it will have to work in the short as well as long terms. It will need to be able to deal with wholes within which parts can be integrated.

Planning ideas are now in considerable disarray. The increasing pressures of technology (mobility and mass production are the two aspects of technology which immediately affect environment) have created almost automatically a social and physical form which can be summed up in the words 'Los Angeles': the city, or non-city, of sprawling suburbs held together by super-highways; a way of life conditioned by the car, for transportation, and television, for entertainment. Both inventions create and sustain individual and family isolation at the environmental level while providing a compensatory shadow participation in the macro-world. Thus total awareness of world events coexists with total ignorance of even one's immediate surroundings. At the same time there is an appalled realization that we have unwittingly lost irreplaceable treasures, discarded irrecoverable aesthetic and social pleasures for the benefits of an ephemeral technology.

The theories on which modern planning is based are descended

The necessary monument

from the preoccupation with public health in the nineteenth
century. They are basically preventive, and negative. The modern
movement in architecture brought to this body of expertise a
concern for logic, for precision and for equality that fitted precisely
with the technological and social preoccupations of the 'twenties.
In those early days of mass production the processes of manu-
facture were continually subdivided, and simplified: 'piece-work',
a very revealing definition. This organizational technique, applied
to cities, produces a set of tests and rules for new buildings: light
angles, plot ratios, density allowances, zoning areas, added to the
existing sanitary regulations. The resulting product, like the
equivalent end result of early mechanization in other fields, was an
introvert and hermetic object, economically and structurally
self-sufficient, and of course, inevitably, architecturally independent
and self-regarding. The ideal city image was a collection of
buildings camping in a public park. Every element in the problem
that the planner, the developer or the architect could control was
pushed toward this technical solution; and none could foresee the
social and aesthetic cost that would have to be paid.

This account must now be settled. We find ourselves in cities
almost destroyed by our own adherence to such primitive logic.
Technology has moved on and is now quite unconcerned with
products any more. It is now concerned with systems, with
processes, with connections between processes. A new generation
of planning theorists is not far behind, adapting the methodology
and computer games, with equally little concern for things felt and
seen, or for the users who have to live and work in the resulting
environment.

In this flux of theoretical change, and with the humbling example
of our theories being demonstrated (in a very short space of time)
to be thoroughly inadequate, we must realistically hang on to what
we have, and try to perceive its value. Propagandists of modern
architecture rewrote history to prove the inadequacy of our
predecessors, choosing a line of development that would lead
logically to our revered pioneers – Gropius, le Corbusier and Mies
van der Rohe – and denigrating those who would not fit the
theory. Thus we withdrew intellectual support from the non-
conforming architects of the past, and made no protest when their
buildings were threatened or butchered, or when architecturally
unfashionable areas were 'redeveloped'. Once a pattern of
disrespect is established it is very difficult to eradicate, as we can
also observe in many other fields.

Our pervasive communications system, too, works against us in
many subtle ways. Theory, opinion and controversy are circulated
rapidly and widely from the centres where controversy seems to
originate, a few great cities. In the context of these cities the

The Necessary Monument

opposition, and stability, of the intellectual audience provides a damping effect, and nothing drastic seems to happen. The argument is simply part of the game of city life. In areas of less dense intellectual involvement, however, the effect is to cancel out existing opinion, and promote intellectual insecurity. An example: the development of the Costa Brava in Spain, where an international commercial modernism has undermined and destroyed a perfectly adequate provincial tradition of building, in itself a major attraction of the area.

In places without tradition, but with a dynamic economy, such as Los Angeles, any innovation or new ideology is acceptable, and technology runs free, to establish the natural form of the corporate society. There is nothing to lose, and perhaps something dramatic to gain. Such is not the case in mature cities, where technology can be recognized as only one of many shaping forces. Here the existing structures, whether intellectual, physical, social or economic, are more able to resist or to incorporate radical concepts.

'An architecture of our time' has always been a radical concept. To promote it now requires a realization that, after sixty years of pioneering, we must take a wider, more inclusive view, to test the present in the context of the past as well as the hopeful future.

This book is an attempt to follow a single thread towards a new method of looking at and dealing with cities. It tries to isolate a single element in the marvellously complex fabric and to *see* it; and to share the enormous pleasure of discovery. It is not original; it is not inventive; our awakening to the importance of nineteenth-century architecture has been initiated by Nikolaus Pevsner, and many others less persuasive; the social consequences of technology on cities have been explored by Jane Jacobs and William H. Whyte, to whose works I owe a great deal.

The Paris Opéra: a monument reborn

When General de Gaulle came to power in 1959 France was deeply divided, sapped by long and pointless wars in Vietnam and Algeria, and technologically backward. De Gaulle's strategy of renouncing the French Empire and concentrating on building a powerful and independent nation has proved masterly. By lavish expenditure on the newest technologies he changed the direction of the economy. Very soon this investment began to pay off in terms of Mirage bombers and nuclear power, but also — more importantly — in the creation of the technostructure which organizes and produces these things. In a remarkably short time France closed the technological gap. The roads, however energetically rebuilt, cannot today contain the vast numbers of cars; the cities are crammed with countrymen seeking the affluent life; computer programmers lurk at every corner.

Within five years de Gaulle had changed the spirit of his country from anxiety and depression, to security and confidence. In fact, the imposition of the new problems of affluence on the volatile and intelligent French brought inevitably the crisis of conscience of the student uprisings, and the equally predictable indifference of the workers. In the crises of mature capitalism, idealist youth sides with the underprivileged; the well-paid worker identifies with the technostructure.

Within the strategy to contain the larger social problems, however, de Gaulle produced a host of intelligent tactics to focus the attention of his countrymen on the building and renovation of France. Apart from expenditure on technology (dams, nuclear power stations, a rocket programme, atomic submarines and the usual defence apparatus of the advanced countries) there are in hand enormous programmes for regional transformation, new towns, and above all, the restructuring of Paris.

No country is so focused on its capital as France. Here are the schools, the institutes, the concentrated apparatus of government. Above all, Paris is the symbol of France. The decision to clean the buildings of the capital was simple, brave and intelligent. It was such a direct and obvious thing to do, but it went against a century of traditional grubbiness, when to paint your mansion was to invite a visit from the tax man. The government set an example, cleaning its own buildings, including the churches which had been nationalized in 1790. Area by area the city has been cleansed, individual owners persuaded, bribed or threatened into conformity.

The results are nothing short of miraculous. Paris is revealed as the most beautiful city in the world.

At the same time programmes for the conservation of historic areas

Left: east pavilion of the south front of the Opéra. Note the effortless integration of diverse and complex elements of architecture and sculpture

The Paris Opera: a monument reborn

were set in motion, in Paris and other cities. In Paris the Marais, the seventeenth-century area around the Place des Vosges, is being quietly renovated, the palaces restored and converted to flats and appartments.

Initially the money for conservation comes from the state, through a characteristic maze of quasi-public corporations which also involves banks and building societies. Since the consequences of sustained investment have become apparent, private money has flooded in. The Marais has become fashionable, and the state and its partners have an excellent investment.

Part of the first phase of the cleaning programme were the great monuments: the Louvre, Notre Dame, the Madeleine and the Opéra. Each is revealed as an architectural miracle which our generation is privileged to see as no one has seen them for a century. Of these the most surprising is the Opéra.

The Nouvel Opéra de Paris was the greatest work of Charles Garnier, whose bust stands outside the west door. It is perhaps the prototypical academic building. Precisely within the main tradition of the Ecole des Beaux-Arts, it gave that tradition a powerful impetus and ensured the dominance of French classicism

Right: general view and left, detail from the south front

The Paris Opera: a monument reborn

for fifty years. Jean-Louis Charles Garnier* was born in 1825 and was a student of Levéil, Lebas and the Ecole des Beaux-Arts. At the Ecole he won the Grand Prix de Rome in architecture in 1848, and spent his years at the French Academy in Rome measuring Roman remains and Renaissance monuments. At this time the sixth-century temple of Zeus at Aegina was discovered. It was remarkably complete, retaining much of its polychromy, and Garnier produced the influential publication drawings. After journeys to Constantinople and Sicily he returned to Paris, to work for the department of public works. Always a superb draughtsman, his professional debut was to win, at the age of thirty-six, the competition for the Opéra, against 171 competitors in the first stage and four others in the second.

---

* Garnier's subsequent works included the Casino at Monte Carlo, the church and school at Bordighera, the Casino, baths, and hotel at Vittel, numerous villas, the tombs of Bizet, Offenbach and Victor Masse. At the Paris Exposition of 1889 he was the consulting architect. He died in 1898 loaded with honours: member of the Institut de France, Grand Officer of the Legion of Honour, RIBA Royal Gold Medallist etc., etc.

Above: the gilt bronze bust of Garnier outside the west carriage entrance
Left and right: details of the south front

The Paris Opéra: a monument reborn

The new building was destined to fill a space that had been painstakingly prepared by Rouhalt de Fleury and Henri Blondel in 1858. The Place de l'Opéra is remarkably plain and severe, in the coldest neo-classic style, and the surrounding palaces perfectly contrast with the exuberant polychromy and formal complexity of Garnier's building. The Opéra is in many ways curiously un-French and was much maligned at the time of its construction. It was considered squat, vulgar and garish, though everyone accepted its powerful imagery and recognized its virtues. Even today the building comes as a shock. Blinded by familiarity with all the world's buildings as we are, we can never recapture the impact that this great building had when it was opened in January 1875, fourteen years after the first stones were laid. Though the building was virtually finished in 1870, the Franco-Prussian war delayed completion. Ironically, the building most associated with the style of Napoleon III was never visited by the Emperor.

Left: the main public entrance.
Garnier designed or supervised the superb bronze lamps, railings and other decorative elements which complement the building
Below: the Opéra circa 1908

21

The Paris Opéra: a monument reborn

Above: the salon over the east entrance

Left: the east carriageway entrance

Below left: detail of the south front

Below: the shadowed north front

The style is more Italian than French, in its rich modelling and in its three-dimensional plasticity. The way Garnier used arcades, through which vistas and further architectural elements can be seen, owed much to Piranesi; and the whole splendid tumbling edifice is massed, with contrasting volumes starting from the arcaded façade, through the dome of the auditorium to the tall scenery tower, with a Baroque exuberance. The order and clarity of its organization is best appreciated on the plan. In walking around the building one is more conscious of the sculptural control, the rich plasticity of the façades, and the sheer invention of the detailing. It is not archaeological. In the spiky forms which contrast with the classical mouldings, there is more than an echo of the Art Nouveau which was to come in the 'nineties. Each front has its major feature which draws the eye: the south entrance is arcaded and richly shadowed, dominating the immense Avenue de l'Opéra cut through to the Louvre in 1878. The west front is pompous with ramped carriageways for the Emperor's coach. Here the decoration takes on an added luxuriance: caryatides and eagles abound, all freely articulated within a tight architectural control. The north front is flat, shadowed and gloomily impressive and the east has another important entrance under a dome.

The Paris Opéra: a monument reborn

Above and right: details of one of
the bronze lights, a perfect example
of Second Empire style
Left: details of the entrance on the
west front; the sheer virtuousity of
the carving is breathtaking

Following pages: cross section and
elevation of the Opéra, from the
publication drawings which are
perhaps the finest ever produced
for any building

Coupe sur la Salle

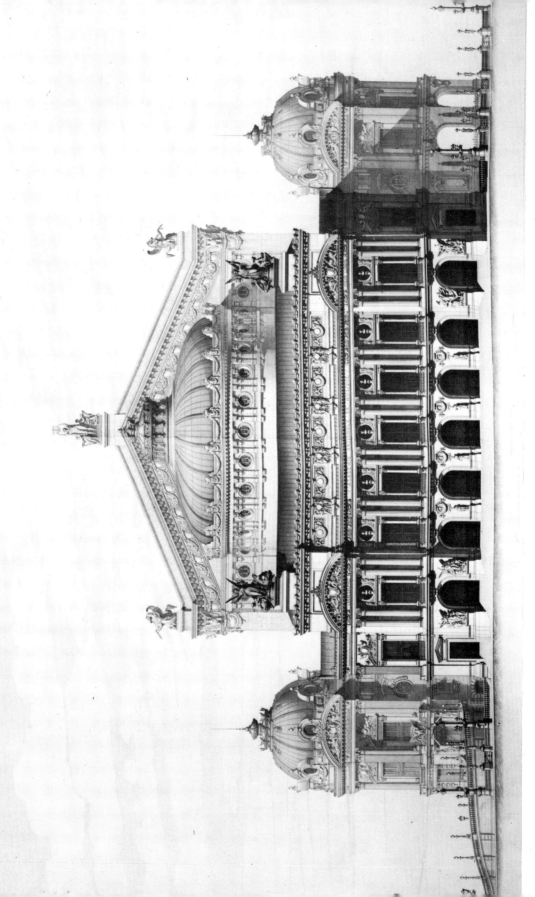

The Paris Opéra: a monument reborn

The interior is a brilliant sequence of extraordinarily complex spaces, interpenetrating each other, offering galleries, stairs and promenades to see and to be seen. The spectators are all actors in a stage set where everyone plays his most elegant role.

The interior decoration is incredibly rich and complex, and always inventive. Throughout the building one feels the presence of painters and sculptors. Their work (capitals, murals, complex mouldings, mosaic floors and sculptural groups) organized and systematized by the architect, adds to but is not dominated by the architecture. Such an integration of the arts, possible within a coherent aesthetic philosophy such as that of the Beaux-Arts, seems incredible today. To come upon such a richly worked example is an experience which produces, in the end, despair. In our time the early hopes of the integration of painting and sculpture into modern architecture have come to grief on the commercial gallery system with its premium on artistic individuality and extremism on one side, and the pressures of economy and technology on the other.

Above, below and left: the Grand Escalier d'Honneur
Below right: a ceiling boss in the entrance hall

In the Opéra the technologies of the arts are still in balance, the materials of the artist the same as those of the builder, only richer and more concentrated. Decoration then was not a dirty word. Thus the sculptural groups by Carpeaux, outward going and energetic, are symbolic, in subject and material, of the intention of the building as a whole. It is just this coherence that makes the building particularly valuable, that makes it such a lesson to our fragmented aesthetic. The Opéra stands near the end of an epoch, and incorporates the hard won lessons of 400 years. It is obvious that to achieve a similar wholeness we have to correct many basic tendencies in our culture. This will take time, and perhaps a good deal of blood and tears, but the example of a great extrovert building is highly relevant to the future form of cities.

A monument in balance: Tower Bridge

Tower Bridge is a building that produces an effect on its surroundings infinitely greater than its elemental function as a traffic machine. This is due to its size, and to its complexity as a mechanism, as an element of urban enclosure and as an historical commentary.

It is a large bridge, 142 feet high, literally closing the river from both directions with a web of granite and steel. Without its vertical scale, it could not relate the two river banks to form one of the largest open spaces in London, the Pool. Though the south bank is now greatly decayed, this great enclosure is a model for a city space, filled with incident, with cranes and ships, with a background of glowering warehouses on the south and a sunlit north bank full of splendid buildings: Adelaide House; Wren's St Magnus the Martyr, the Customs House, and above all, the Tower. In this context the bridge far exceeds its function, and becomes an architectural dominant.

Much of its success arises from its intrinsic complexity as a mechanism. Because the roadway must rise to allow for the passage of ocean-going ships, the physical problems within the structure are enormous. Their detailed solution, one of the great triumphs of Victorian engineering, is described in the appendix. Within the context of the city, however, this complexity of use provides the programme for a unique building: a road capable of movement, machine rooms, control offices, living quarters for a working community. In comparison, the simplistic briefs given to the engineers of contemporary motorways are elementary. Because their programmes are elementary, the final results are always dull.

The bridge is in high Victorian Gothic, and stylistically responds to the mediaeval Tower, and self-righteously comments upon it. The sharp, hard, granite detailing mocks the latter's crumbling stones, and the precision and earnest exactitude of the mouldings contrasts with the heavy Romanesque of the Tower. Yet it is a contrast within the same language and largely within the same technology; a twentieth-century architect could possibly produce an equally valid response, but both the language and the technology are irrevocably lost. A complex of social, technological, economic and aesthetic factors now exists which makes it impossible for the bridge ever to be reproduced, or to be repeated. These things also make its continued existence precarious.

The bridge takes its place in a great succession of structures connecting the two banks of London's river. Early inhabitants used the ford at Westminster, and the Romans used a ferry at the site of London Bridge. A timber bridge is mentioned as being in existence in 993, and in 1176 it was proposed, by a chaplain of the church in the Poultry in which Thomas à Beckett was baptised, that a

Left: the Pool of London, between Tower and London Bridges. At right, the Tower of London and St Katharine's Docks, now decayed and awaiting redevelopment

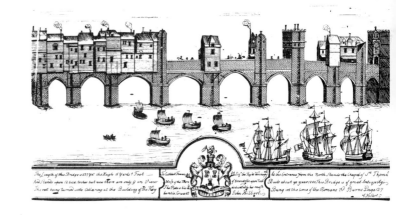

The Length of this Bridge is 374 foot the height 16 yards 1 foot
And Stands upon 12 old arches but now there are only 9 in Vieiw
The rest being turned into Cellaring at the Building of the Key

Sr Iohn Lambert Vintner
Major of the Thire
the Plate is here fixt
humbly forward

Chiefe of the Right Worshipg
of Newcastle upon Tine
dedicated by his maiesty
Iohn Philbert

to the Entrance from the North Stands the Chapel of Sr Thomas
Built about ye year 1200 This Bridge is of great Antiquity
Being in the time of the Romans D° Burns Page 27
I. Philbert.

Die Brücke zu London

A monument in balance: Tower Bridge

stone bridge should be built. This was completed by 1209, and the first London Bridge survived for 700 years. It was 926 feet long, 40 feet wide and near the middle, a span was opened by a drawbridge. The bridge was supported by nineteen arches, on piers 25-34 feet thick, carried on elm piles driven into the bed of the river. On the tenth pier was a chapel dedicated to St Thomas of Canterbury, and thus began the habit of building other structures integral with the bridge. (There were many other contemporary examples.) A tower was built on the north side in 1426, and houses from 1471. They were probably of timber, and burnt down in 1632 and 1666, but were always rapidly rebuilt.

Above left: the mediaeval bridge at Newcastle upon Tyne followed the pattern of old London Bridge
Left: London Bridge in 1735. Note the elegant and orderly structures resulting from the rebuilding of 1666, and the relation to the tower of St Magnus Martyr, whose porch marked the north end of the bridge

The funds for maintaining the bridge came from endowments of land, and from the revenue of the chapel. As these lands steadily increased in value over the centuries, their revenue has grown hugely. The Bridge House Estates have been able to rebuild London Bridge, build Blackfriars Bridge, and Tower Bridge, and to buy and allow free public use of Southwark Bridge. As Tower Bridge cost £902,500, excluding the cost of the land, a very considerable sum in 1895, the extent of the Bridge House Estates investments can be imagined.

Old London Bridge caused a tremendous blockage of the river. Its close-set piers, which were thickened from time to time with timber outworks to protect the piles on which it was built, formed a weir, so that the tide flow was considerably impeded. There was, even in an unexceptional tide, a difference of 5 feet between water level on either side of the bridge, making the passage under the bridge an exciting and dangerous undertaking. The flow of water was used in 1582, when water wheels were erected under the arches at the north end, to pump London's water supply. The stabilizing effect of the barrier on the upper reaches must have been considerable, making the use of the river much easier than it is now, and reducing the wear and scour on the banks.

The spans of old London Bridge varied from 10 to 30 feet and as ships grew bigger the need for a larger opening became apparent. An arch 70 feet wide was made in the centre of the span in 1759; some houses were cleared even earlier to make a proper carriage road. In the end the pressure of coach traffic became overwhelming. A new structure by Sir Charles Rennie was opened in 1831, at a cost of £1,500,000. This was well proportioned and beautiful, but a simple carriageway, and in its turn it was demolished in 1967 and transported to Lake Havasu City, Arizona, USA, one of the larger souvenirs. The newest bridge is an undistinguished motorway, though a separate pedestrian bridge is being provided at a higher level.

A monument in balance: Tower Bridge

It is an interesting comment that the iron bridges of the Thames, such as Tower Bridge, all turned out to be very much cheaper to build than the traditional stone bridges. They also retained their value to a greater extent when their private owners were bought out by the government in the late nineteenth century. London Bridge was sold for 2·46 million dollars (just under a million pounds in 1967).

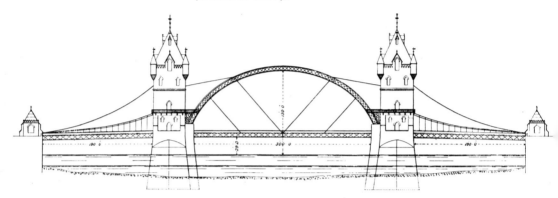

The vast growth of South and East London during the late nineteenth century produced an increasing demand for more bridges,* but the overriding requirements of the Board of the Thames Conservancy for free river access for ocean-going ships prevented any conventional solution east of London Bridge.

Sir Marc Isambard Brunel proposed a tunnel between Wapping and Rotherhithe in 1824, and after immense difficulties it was opened to pedestrians in 1843. The idea of vehicular traffic had to be abandoned because of the mounting expenses (£468,000) and the tunnel was afterwards sold to the East London Railway Company. Trains still use it.

The next move was the Tower Subway, an iron tube 7 feet in diameter from Great Tower Hill on the west side of the Tower to Pickle Herring Stairs on the south bank. This was opened in 1871 for pedestrians, and in spite of long access stairways nearly a million people used it each year, at a toll of $\frac{1}{2}$d for each passage.

In May 1877 the City Architect, Sir Horace Jones, reported to his Bridge Committee on the alternative possibilities of the Tower Bridge site, and in the following year put forward the idea of the bascule bridge which after much argument was to find acceptance.

---

* A survey in August 1882 of London Bridge produced the daily user figures of 22,242 vehicles and 110,525 pedestrians, on a bridge only 54 feet wide.

A monument in balance: Tower Bridge

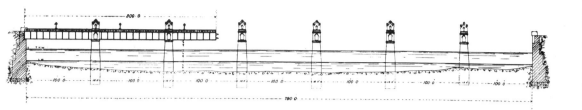

Above: Sir George Barclay Bruce's proposal of 1876 for a mechanical ferry
Left: Sir Horace Jones's first design for Tower Bridge in 1878, the basic idea for the final structure
Below: E. J. Palmer's proposal of 1877 for a double 'Duplex' bridge

In 1876 however Sir George Bruce had proposed a rolling bridge, a platform 300 feet × 100 feet which would move across a series of piers 100 feet apart. These would contain the rollers and driving machinery to propel this ingenious mechanical ferry from bank to bank.

An equally complex solution was the 'Duplex' Bridge, by F. J. Palmer, in 1877, which was a forerunner of another related proposal put up by a private company in 1884. Palmer's bridge consisted of two locks, with sliding spans to allow shipping to enter the lock; the span would then be closed, allowing vehicular traffic to move, while the alternative span slid away to allow the ship to move on. The complexity, and the small spaces available for the ships, made the idea unworkable.

A monument in balance: Tower Bridge

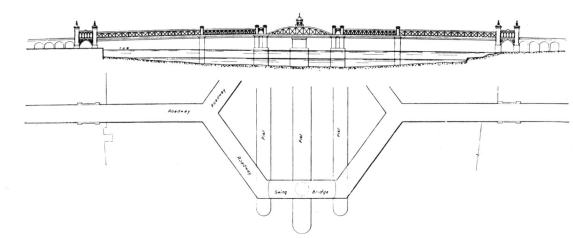

Above: the single 'Duplex' design by Bell and Miller, 1884
Below: the plan of Sir Joseph Bazalgette's proposals for a medium level bridge, showing the 5000 foot spiral southern approach gradient. The plan also shows the traditional method of mooring ships in tiers.

The revised proposal of 1884 had only a single lock, in the centre of the river, with double movable roadways at each end. Here again the width of the lock, and the cumbersome road approach, would have caused a great obstruction to river traffic.

The Metropolitan Board of Works applied to Parliament in 1879 to build a magnificent medium level bridge, designed by Sir Joseph Bazalgette, with an arched single span of 850 feet and a 65 feet clearance above high water. It would have been a wonderful structure, but involved great problems of access — particularly on the south side where a 5,700 feet long spiral ramp was proposed. (Sir Joseph had produced, on the same basic plan and approach system, two alternative designs, in 1878. They were for a cantilever, and for a lattice girder bridge.) The wharfingers, however, thought the clearance inadequate, and the idea was abandoned.

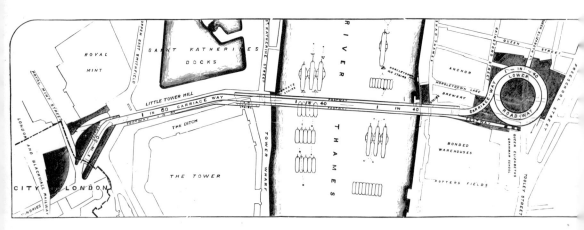

A monument in balance: Tower Bridge

Above: Sir Joseph Bazalgette's
famous design for a single span
steel arch bridge which he produced
in 1878
Below: alternative designs for cantilever and lattice girder bridges, with
pier supports in the river, proposed
by Sir Joseph in the same year. All
three bridges would have used the
same basic plan and approach level.

A monument in balance: Tower Bridge

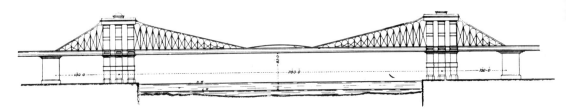

Above: an elegant medium level
single span cantilever design by A.
J. Sedley, 1879

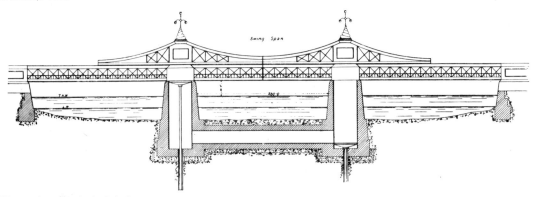

Above: the most logical design, a
swing span by Knipple and Morris,
1884. Pedestrians would descend
by lifts to a tunnel

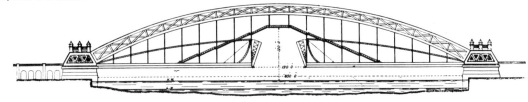

Above: a single-arched low level
span, with bascules, by Ordish and
Matheson, 1885

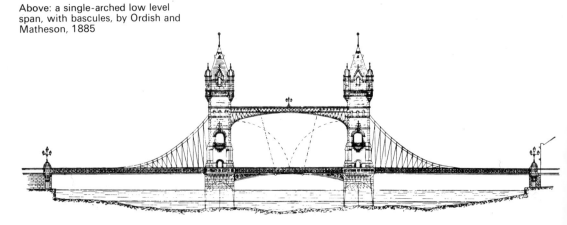

A monument in balance: Tower Bridge

In the 1883 Parliamentary session a private company proposed a tunnel, served by 'large and numerous hydraulic lifts', only to be opposed by the Metropolitan Board of Works, who produced their own plans for a tunnel the following year. This one had mile-long ramp approaches on both banks, and involved tremendous land acquisition costs.

The confusion caused by two very different proposals produced the usual parliamentary committee to examine the whole problem. After much consideration they decided that a low level bridge, with minimum problems of approach ramping, with an opening span, should be developed, and asked the City of London to undertake the work.

This naturally brought the job to the Bridge House Estates Committee who, after appointing a deputation to visit the continent, Newcastle upon Tyne and other places with opening bridges, recommended Sir Horace Jones's original idea of 1878 for a bascule bridge.

His first proposal was for a steel arched structure over the main span, with main river piers very much as they are today, but in a rather French style. The difficulty was that the arched form did not allow the bascules to open completely, so that ships would be forced to stay precisely in the centre of the opening — which was a good deal to ask of sailing ships in a strong tide.

Sir Wolfe Barry was appointed as engineer for the bridge in 1884, and Sir Horace Jones as architect, and the impact of a fresh mind became at once apparent. The arch was dropped and a straight span substituted. The bascules could now open vertically, leaving the entire 200 feet span clear for shipping.

The revised design was approved by Parliament in 1885, and the long process of detail designing began.

Yours faithfully, J Wolfe Barry

Above: portrait of Sir John Wolfe Barry
Left: the design by Jones and Barry approved by Parliament in 1885

The way in which the river was used at that time provided the basic layout. Vessels were moored in two, or sometimes three, parallel lines, head to stern, on either side of the river, leaving a clear 200-250 feet fairway down the middle. Goods were unloaded into barges for transport up river or to the bankside quays and warehouses.

Because the river use was relatively static some distance out from the banks, it was clear that the opening span need not be greater than the 200 feet wide fairway, with two side openings of some 300 feet which could be at a low level. Thus the position of the river piers was soon determined. In spite of the logic, the bridge

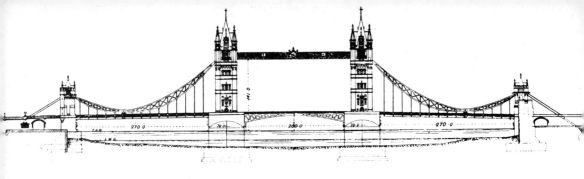

Above: the completed bridge by Sir John Wolfe Barry

Opposite and following pages: a selection of the architectural working drawings prepared by George D. Stevenson

was opposed by river users and the Conservancy and only passed through Parliament with several stringent conditions. The main requirements were that 160 feet of the central fairway should be kept open at all times (making it impossible to build more than one pier foundation at a time) and that the bridge be opened for two hours at high tide (which caused the elaborate provision of lifts and stairs for pedestrians to pass over at high level).

Because of the recent Tay Bridge disaster (1879), the Board of Trade required that all new structures be able to withstand wind pressures of 56 pounds per square foot; so that the mechanical provisions in the moving spans are somewhat excessive. The machinery required to work against this pressure was duplicated in each pier.

Parliament defined the opening span as 200 feet clear, 135 feet clearance above Trinity High Water when open and 29 feet when closed. The river piers were to be 185 feet long and 70 feet wide. Side spans were to be 270 feet clear.

Work began on 21st June 1886. The government allowed a small encroachment on the Tower Ditch, and in return required that the architecture of the bridge should accord with the Tower. Their other condition, that the bridge might be armed with guns, was afterwards abandoned, until an anti-aircraft battery was established on the river piers in 1940.

Sir Horace Jones intended a somewhat feudal architectural expression, in brick with stone dressings, and thought of the bridge working like a drawbridge in a castle, with chains. When Sir Wolfe came on the scene the engineering problems were critical and architectural considerations were put aside until the basic mechanisms were decided and the foundations were under way. Sir Horace died in 1887, before any architectural detail had been decided, and Sir Wolfe took control entirely. The programme had been much changed and, apart from the original concept, there is no doubt that the bridge owes its form and its mechanisms to Barry. It has an engineering straightforwardness that runs through all the details, and the precision and pedantry of the architecture is characteristic of the Victorian engineer. His architectural assistant, Mr Stevenson, was very much a part of a larger team of specialists.

TOWER BRIDGE
Elevation of East & West fronts Main Towers
10 20 30 40 50 60 70 80 90 100 feet
Scale of Feet
High Water Line
Architect

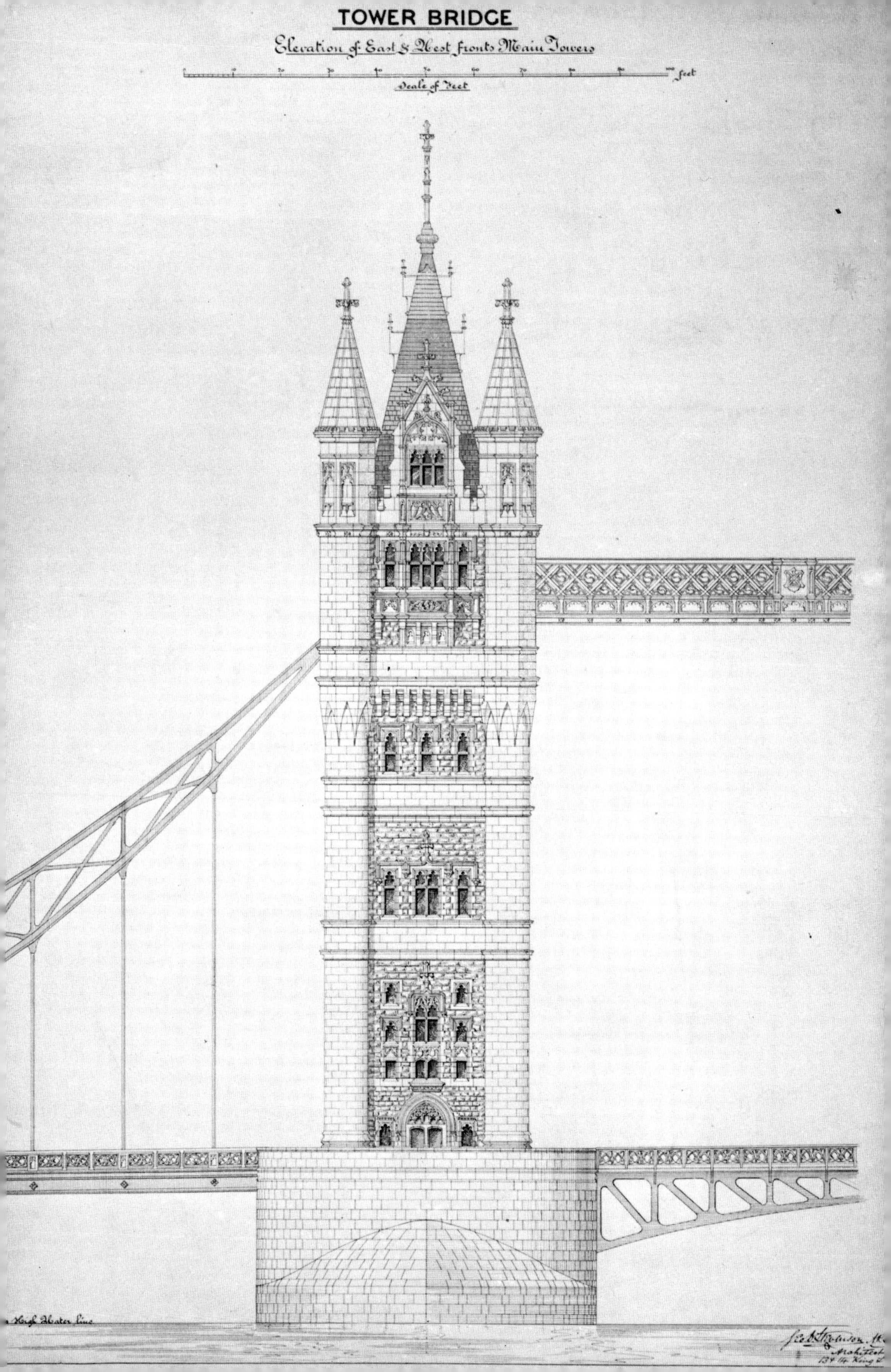

TOWER BRIDGE

— Elevation of Main Towers facing Land ~~~ —

Scale of feet

TOWER BRIDGE

Detail of Top Stage East & West fronts of Main Towers

Scale of Feet

— Elevation —   Rock faced Granite

Section on Centre Line

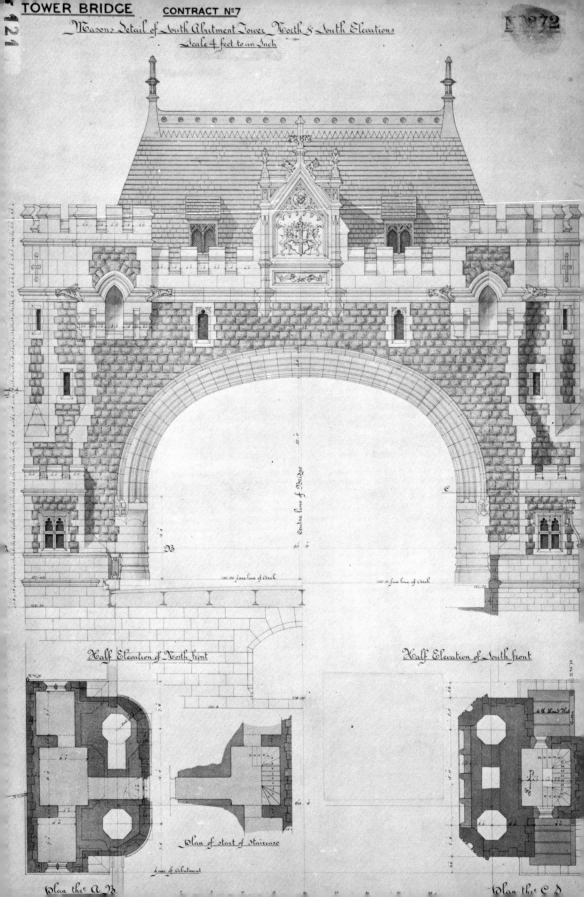

Half Elevation of North Front

Half Elevation of South Front

Plan of start of Staircase

Plan thro' A.B.

Plan thro' C.D.

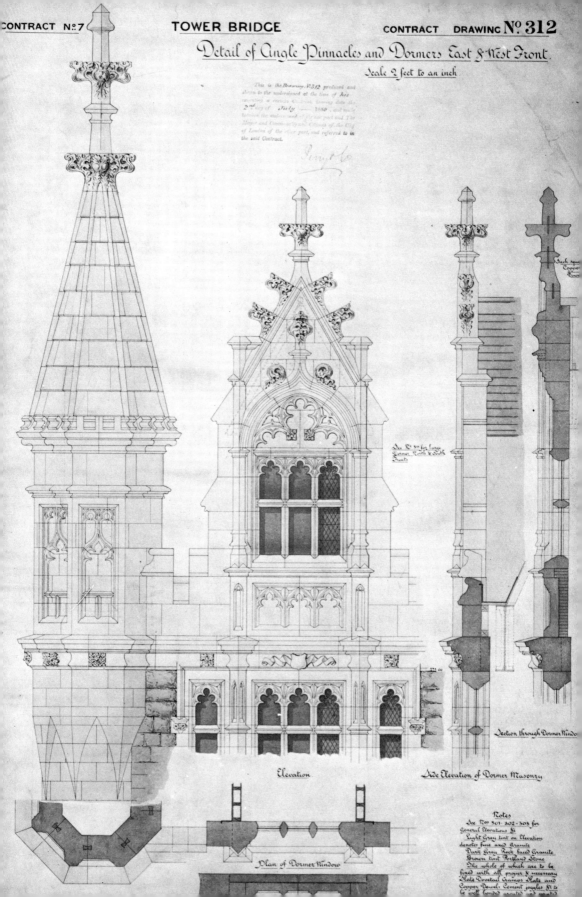

Detail of Angle Pinnacles and Dormers East & West Front.

Scale 2 feet to an inch

This is the Drawing No. 312 produced and
shewn to the undersigned at the time of his
executing a certain Contract, bearing date the
2nd day of July ——— 1889 ——— and made
between the undersigned of the one part and The
Mayor and Commonalty and Citizens of the City
of London of the other part, and referred to in
the said Contract.

See No. 311 for larger
Dormer North & South
Fronts

See No. —— for Corner
Cross

Elevation

Side Elevation of Dormer Masonry

Section through Dormer Window

Plan of Dormer Window

Notes

See Nos. 301. 302. 303. for
General Elevations &c
Light Grey tint on Elevation
denotes fine and Granite
Dark Grey Rock faced Granite
Brown tint Portland Stone
The whole of which are to be
fixed with all proper & necessary
Slate Dovetail Cramps Slate and
Copper Dowels Cement joggles &c &c
to be well bonded grouted and

Tower Bridge today

Except at the south end, Tower Bridge shows few signs of wear or decay, though its surroundings are very much in process of change. On the north side, east of the Tower, is St Katharine's Docks, one of the great masterpieces of Victorian building, designed by Thomas Telford. These splendid warehouses, resting on Doric cast-iron columns, surround an enclosed pool, with lock gates to the river. They have been empty for many years and the future of the group has been in dispute. Because of their relatively small scale, the narrowness of the access lock and the now obsolete methods of handling cargo, they have shared the general decay of upriver docking. Andrew Renton's proposals for their intelligent redevelopment, with housing, offices and an entertainment complex, are very welcome. The basins become a yacht marina, and it is to be hoped that the artists, at present in one block, will remain.

Above: the bridge from the Tower terrace
Above left: the west side with the brewery behind
Left: view from the east
Above right: the proposed redevelopment of St Katharine's Docks

The bridge itself is in remarkable condition; the original notices are still there, and the control cabins are well maintained, shiplike and tidy. The sensations on the bridge are marvellously complex, the web of steel against the sky, the vibration underfoot, the traffic on the roadway and, on the other side of the great thick balustrade, the river, boats and birds. The air of excitement and participation is a liberation of the spirit.

On the Tower side the riverside garden provides excellent views of the river and the bridge, and the small café there needs only to be lifted from its repulsive and obsolete squalor to become a very pleasant place.

The south side is rather more depressing. The long straight

approach, lined with nondescript buildings, is deflationary. On the west is a maze of bomb-damaged warehouses, which have not been replaced and whose function and value decrease yearly. The whole of this side of the Pool must very soon be rebuilt and the possibility of a mixed industrial, office, housing area with its own character is certainly there. The difficulty is that present planning methodology would almost certainly guarantee a desert of separated uses, and the high land cost makes any kind of more sophisticated intervention difficult. In areas such as this the difficulty of raising adequate capital forces a local authority to auction off its redevelopment rights (compulsory purchase powers) to the highest commercial bidder. In turn the developer, to safe-guard his own position, will provide only those elements (offices, factory space) which produce the highest immediate return. This elementary sequence automatically produces a complex entirely lacking in complexity, without those marginal uses which give nuance, quality and life to an environment. Perhaps we should hopefully wait until the shipping use has resolved itself into a new pattern before making plans, and who knows, by then we may know how to state the problem of redevelopment correctly.

The southeast side of the bridge is dominated by the large Courage Brewery which, like most breweries, is a maze of alterations and additions that give a pleasantly romantic skyline.

Above: the memorial stone on the north side
Above right: the bridge seen from the Tower
Right: the north approach

At this side, too, is the main accumulator house (see page 117), a simple cube of brickwork — a little drab perhaps — but intended to be read as part of the street rather than of the bridge. Beside it is a stair down to the roadway under the Surrey approach, which leads to the boilers and engine room. Here the maintenance is somewhat less respectful. This working area shares the squalor we have come to think of as inherent in work, and has its origin perhaps in the handling of coal. An elaborate system of hydraulic cranes was provided to lift coal from barges to small railway trucks, which then ran to the coal store in an arch between the engines and the boilers. When the floor was filled with coal, the trucks were raised by an hydraulic lift to an overhead conveyor running the length of the store, tipping on either side. As coal is now delivered by road the mess is somewhat greater and the servicing more haphazard. The boundary to the west is poorly defined by a bombed warehouse.

The upper works of the towers are little used. The river piers are empty halls over the roadway, and the shore piers contain, on the north side, flats for the staff, and on the south side the administration offices.

The vibration of the traffic makes the use of the accommodation difficult, and the staff prefer to live away from the job.

Above: detail of the north shore
tower
Right: The north shore tower seen
through the arch of the river pier

Above: the north suspension span
with Telford's St Katharine's Docks
beyond
Right: detail of a window in the
river tower

Tower Bridge today

Above: the north west control cabin
Right: detail of the suspension
chain
Far right: connection of suspension
span to the balustrade
Below: signal at the control cabin

Above: detail of the City Coat of
Arms over the shore towers
Right: a detail of the river tower

Above: the pinnacles on the river
towers with the high level bridge
Right: a niche and window in the
south river tower

Junctions of steel and stone
Above: the housing of the
suspension span into the shore
towers
Right: the tie from the Surrey bank
to the shore tower
Far right: the suspension span
housed into the river tower

A page of details
Above: a finial over a river tower niche
Right: a lintel on the river tower
Above right: carving at the base of a
niche

NO ADMITTANCE
XCEPT ON BUSINESS

Above: notice at the control cabin
Right: sign at the north tower arch

FOOT
PASSENGERS
MUST NOT PASS
THRO' THE ARCH

Above: view from the bridge southeast to the picturesque Courage
Brewery
Far right: a detail of the massive
connection to the suspension span
Right: gantry at the control cabin,
with fine cast iron railings

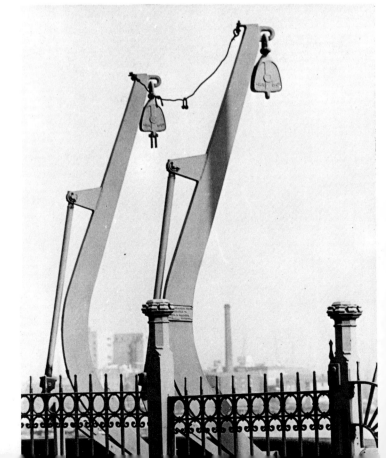

The social connection

Perhaps the most valuable of Tower Bridge's functions is one which it fulfills badly, but which it inherits, as no other Thames crossing, from Old London Bridge. Tower Bridge is still a place to walk on; it invites a crossing by its promise of a complex architectural experience, its promise of something shared: a marvellous series of views up and down stream, a participation in the working life of the river (as opposed to the working life of the streets which other bridges convey), and an involvement in the drama of the Pool. The latter is a complex socio-historic phenomenon: big ships, cranes, Customs House, Tower, St Magnus Martyr, Billingsgate, the tottering warehouses. The sensations of participating in history, in the activity of the Fish Market, in the work and life of the ships and seamen are deliciously interwoven. This multitude of experiences, intricately and subconsciously overlaid, is the very stuff of cities, the product of a rich mix of uses and associations, and itself the justification of the romantic view of cities. It is the rewarding end product of complexity (and it has also a very real cash value).

It is this quality of participation that Tower Bridge has inherited from Old London Bridge. The latter was at once a barrier to shipping (it marked the limit for ocean-going ships) and a barrage for the tide. The effect was to slow down tidal change above the bridge and produce a higher and more stable water level, which in turn helped the users of the river and ensured an equalizing growth on both banks. The river was not a barrier in the way it became in the nineteenth century and remains today, though there was only one bridge for 700 years. In fact, the provision of other bridges was strenuously resisted by the City of London merchants.

Old London Bridge was primarily a shopping street. This extra use provided a permanent and highly sophisticated value link between the two banks. Above the shops were houses, including many famous and beautiful buildings, so that the continuity of the city was virtually uninterrupted from side to side.

All this has gone, to be replaced only by a series of windy carriageways. The lack of this lifeline, this vital link, is probably the main cause of the catastrophic decline of the south bank in the nineteenth century. And it is certain that nothing will regrow that depressed area until some similar connection is made to the north shore. The creation of a series of cultural monoliths, isolated in a few acres of concrete, will solve nothing, and produce nothing except a demand for more subsidies.

It is the intervention of commercial life, of individual initiatives in creating the small elements of identity that establishes a living city.

The social connection

Above: one of the control
cabins, of which there are four, one
on each side of the river piers

This means shops, large or small, which in some way relate to
their surroundings. Thus any major city element, a museum or
library, will attract shops and pubs that relate to it, and intensify
its own identity. Theatres produce costumiers, wig makers, lighting
specialists. Concert halls create music and instrument shops.
Large public projects that make no provision for this kind of
participation seal themselves into sterile packs: London's south
bank is an example and there are dozens in America, of which
Lincoln Center is only the biggest elephant.

Old London Bridge, which died in 1824 to be replaced by Rennie's
beautiful but elementary structure, could also be considered as a
prototypical route-building, a connector element in the city and a
major encloser of space. Its position as first bridge would have
made the space open ended downstream, so that the strong sense
of enclosure experienced today was lacking. On the other hand,
the river was more used, a maze of vessels and rigging. Its relation
to the Church of St Magnus Martyr, whose porch was on the east
pavement of the bridge and whose tower signalled the city, was
singularly beautiful and poetic.

The realignment of the bridge approach at a higher level further
upstream has destroyed the church, wedged behind a marine
warehouse and office block, and this must be counted a major
loss. But it is still there, a grace note, and an element of history
and poignancy in the scene.

The bridge carried a great variety of houses, with shops under-
neath. Although they were several times burnt, the shops were
quickly rebuilt; and they were probably much altered and adapted
as time went on. Many were famous examples of the architecture
of the period, including Nonsuch House.

Though Tower Bridge has something of this quality of an artery, of
a connection, it has nothing with which to connect. The south
bank is exceptionally barren just here. It would make an
exceedingly interesting experiment to attempt to grow something
at the south abutment, to match the Tower and its garden café
on the other side.

The extraordinary machinery of the bridge, the great pumps and
accumulators, could be a real attraction. The area could be cleaned
up and made visible to spectators. The vast brewery on the east
side might be persuaded to provide a pub, a balcony and a pier
for river craft.

Minimal expenditure perhaps, but a link in a chain of social and
economic value.

Above and below left: one of the great engines in the boiler room under the south approach. The beautiful and well maintained machines, brightly painted, are some of the few remaining examples of Victorian mechanical engineering, and should be one of the sights of London

In making this kind of gesture to the south bank the possibility of a civilized redevelopment of that depressed area becomes closer. The long term profitability of an area depends, ultimately, on its social dynamic and self-regenerative capacity. To rebuild everything every twenty years places a tremendous strain on capital formation. Our tendency towards larger and larger units, in business and in building, makes us forget that the economic problems of replacement, as well as of maintenance, are not eased by increase of scale. When an individual or a small organization might make an impact on a city, with a single building, or even by a redecoration, the burden and benefit of urban growth can be widely spread. Thus a small scale area with many varied owners and users will always by its cycle of random cleaning, painting and alteration demonstrate its inner dynamic, and because of the multiplicity of parts it is less liable to a general blight. Individual operators are seldom all equally affected by single economic factors. Large organizations, on the other hand, which follow the monopolizing trend in our technology, are singularly unprepared for adverse economic trends. They retreat and retrench. It is just this scale of big business, national rather than local, which is inevitably irresponsible at the environmental level. It could hardly be otherwise. The directors of national or international

The social connection

companies are too concerned with the macro-scale to think of the effect on local values their operations may have. They are not concerned with places, but with balance sheets that plot the profitability of their properties. That is, their concern with building is simplistic, purely economic. When a company is swallowed by a large corporation its local ties and responsibilities are cut, its buildings suddenly become unreal. They are no longer the responsibility of a proud founder, but of an administrator concerned with standardization and economy. In any case the current mode of thinking about environmental problems by big corporations – prestige headquarters controlling a scattered empire of sordid back-street factories – makes their involvement dangerous.

Sensitive areas in cities (and nearly all areas in cities are sensitive because people live in them), are therefore best removed from the world of the big company.* Cities are seedbeds, and they grow enterprises. In the early stages of company growth, the firm needs local support and services. With success it can move outwards to larger, more logically arranged premises. But to attempt to pre-empt the seedbed itself for its mature life is a sure way of reducing future growth, and enterprise, in the neighbourhood.

Thus the planning agency is confronted with a dichotomy. On one side the corporations can raise capital and be trusted with large areas of redevelopment, though the end result is guaranteed sterile.†

---

* Corporations: the big grow much bigger.
'The very largest companies are taking over a steadily growing share of US business. Fortune's annual listing last week, published last week, shows that the biggest industrial companies rang up almost 64% of all industrial sales in the US last year, up from 62% in 1967 and just over 55% a decade ago. In their fields the 500 employed 687 out of every 1,000 workers and accounted for 74% of total profits. Despite the tax surcharge, profits were up 13%, to $24 billion.
General Motors again led the list, followed in the top ten by Standard Oil (NJ), Ford, General Electric, Chrysler, IBM, Mobil Oil, Texaco, Gulf Oil and US Steel. Collectively, the top ten increased earnings by 21%, or double the rate of the other 490 companies.
The trend of the 500 underscores the growing importance of "economies of scale." Size clearly offers the opportunity for more efficient use of equipment and greater market clout.' *Time* May 1969.

† Of the many examples we might quote the Shell Centre in London or the Central Electricity Generating Board complex round St Paul's. An instructive early example is the replacement of the Adams Brothers' Adelphi by Shell-Mex House in the 'thirties, a blow from which the area has not yet recovered.
Almost every US city has been devastated on a much larger scale, in a similar way: the Golden Triangle in Pittsburgh is a vast area of new office blocks without even a decent restaurant; the St Louis downtown waterfront replaced acres of cast iron warehouses with banal glass towers still half empty (no restaurant there either). In Paris, the Gare Montparnasse redevelopment is only a forerunner of what is promised for the Halles in the centre of the city.
For a critique of the new city see *Playtime*, a film by Jacques Tati.

The social connection

On the other there is a tremendous financial gamble if smaller firms are involved. The compromise is inevitably to involve the developer who, backed by the insurance companies, tries to hedge his bet with standard shopfronts suitable only for supermarkets and chain stores, and standard office blocks which he will hope to rent to the government or a corporation.

Perhaps there is no way out of this impossible choice except to reduce the scale of operations to one dictated by actual need, rather than attempting to create a need which may not be there at all. Property development is a gamble, which depends largely on inflation to bring a profit. All economic factors including population and productivity increases would seem to push for higher and higher property values, but in practice it is very difficult to create an area from scratch. Great subtlety in the matter of rents and incentives is required to get tenants, and it may be that more involvement, on the smaller scale, will bring about the stability so necessary in development. Thus a tenant with a stake in the whole, or a complete control over a part, has an involvement which no other form of participation can bring. He brings his life, his heart and mind to his environment.

There is no denying that a process of piecemeal growth, and complex involvement of many people on different conditions, is both difficult, uncertain, and for the developer, unprofitable and tiresome. To be at all possible it requires a small scale of operation, and the renunciation of the great speculative profits of recent years. But the alternatives are more dangerous.

The process of city growth requires participation, and reactions. To begin a chain reaction it is necessary to provide a gesture or trigger from which other decisions can be made. To make the decisions all at once (as in a housing estate) is to anticipate or abort all reaction from the participants: their contribution is thereafter largely negative and often destructive. But the introduction of something other, an element which is random or illogical, may be a good beginning. It is this function which is filled by the monument; and Tower Bridge is an excellent example of a trigger mechanism.

The future of monuments

It is perfectly possible to calculate the capacity of a road with a fair degree of accuracy and it has become obvious that Tower Bridge has reached its limits as a road. It is often jammed. The volume of traffic must, according to all the statistics, regularly increase for many years to come, doubling by 1980.

At the same time, technology makes changes in the bridge's other functions: shipping grows less and less in the Pool: St Katharine's Docks are deserted and the owners of the remaining warehouses would dearly love to replace them with offices.

The tendency in shipping is towards containers, standard units of cargo which can be mechanically handled and stacked. For efficiency, the process requires a large unobstructed area, in order to marshal trucks and trains, for the conveyors and transporters. Such areas are available at Tilbury and Gravesend, with good and improving road and rail access. The London Docks are obsolete and archaic, and their continued existence is due entirely to habit and inertia.

Though no official consideration has been given to the future of the bridge — a highly emotive subject — it is clear that some thought is required. To replace it with a tunnel would solve both the road and river problems in a very characteristically twentieth-century way, by removing both the pain and the pleasure from the situation. It would carry many more vehicles and would not be subject to delays caused by shipping. It would be reasonably economical, but the bridge, its emotive impact and its intangible value, would be lost. Another, more sophisticated, proposal is to build a relief road, or roads, in tunnels further downstream. Traffic is cramped on both sides down river, the banks are lined with decaying warehouses and factories, and many possible connections could be made, which would draw the pressure from the bridge. With sufficient alternative routes a traffic balance may be achieved within its environmental capacity.

Such a policy would maintain one section of the status quo, but would not affect the shipping. It is possible that the gradual disappearance of ocean-going shipping from the Pool will automatically retire the ageing engines of the bridge, and thus neatly solve the problem. It would also be possible to hasten the process by Act of Parliament, closing the Pool, and compensating its present users. The bridge would be left firmly down, and we would once again simplify the problem, and lose a spectacle, the bascules in action.

Left: Tower Bridge is perhaps the only bridge in the world constantly visited by summer tourists

A further alternative would be to depend entirely on relief tunnels for motor traffic, and leave the bridge permanently open only to

The future of monuments

shipping. This puts us neatly into the worst possible situation, reducing the pedestrian use of the bridge to nothing and destroying an adequate, though limited capacity, cross river route, for the sake of a dwindling shipping use.

The logic, therefore, seems to be to hold on to the present structure as long as any basic elements of its use continue, allowing it to function in its original way for as long as possible. Adjustment of road and shipping traffic may be required to keep its environmental balance, but they are slight penalties compared to the massive urban and emotional benefits.

Because Tower Bridge is still in operation, its gradual decline in the face of changing functions can be easily observed. This decline has already been completed in the case of many equally important nineteenth-century monuments. London's Euston Arch and New York's Penn Station have gone; in New York Grand Central Station, and in London St Pancras Railway Station and Gilbert Scott's Foreign Office are still under fire. At the scale of these great buildings, many created and still owned by private enterprise, the individual is helpless. These dinosaurs are too big and too expensive to be dealt with except at government level. Here our literary minded bureaucracy finds itself with a problem for which it is not equipped. There is no tradition of spending money to rescue buildings, and, above all, no imaginative enterprise in infusing such buildings with new life, and new uses.

Well-made buildings, even if they have long since repaid their original capital, are seldom incapable of restoration and renewal. Properly funded and maintained, they are self-regenerating economic organisms, as vast areas of seventeenth-and eighteenth-century London and Paris convincingly prove. The Temple, Belgravia, Regent's Park, the Ile St Louis and vast stretches on both sides of the Seine retain their values, repair themselves, are actually enriched by passing time.

Threatened buildings, such as St Pancras Station, require to be reassessed, and revalued at every level*; alternative uses can be suggested which provide the basis for a new existence, which can then be made a reality only by imaginative financial policies.
In the case of Tower Bridge, the value of the structure as urban decoration is overwhelming, and now far outranks its original traffic functions. It must be the only bridge in the world constantly

---

* St Pancras Station, for example, might make a very adequate exhibition hall, the vast cellars serving as workshops, the hotel public rooms being used for conferences, the bedrooms refurbished, or used as administrative offices.

Above: the south bank of the Pool of London, an area becoming daily more obsolete. The regeneration of this dismal stretch without the declining shipping use will depend on its pedestrian connection to the prosperous north side

Below: the terrace of the Tower

filled with summer visitors, marvelling, and enjoying the views and the place. In a leisure society, this is a tangible and rapidly growing asset.

The Tower of London is one of the world's greatest tourist attractions; apart from the building's romantic history, it houses the Crown Jewels, an unsurpassed collection of armour, and a Romanesque chapel. Much of this value spills over to the bridge and it is very noticeable how many people walk across it, only to be shocked and bored by the inhospitable south bank. Interest tapers off rapidly and the tourist beats a hasty retreat.

It is policy to revitalize the south bank and many ponderous projects are under way further up river. Plans have been put forward for a riverside walk, partly floating, and there is a steady growth in awareness of London's river, as it changes from a commercial to a possible leisure and tourist asset. The great rise in boat ownership, the many proposals for marinas and other facilities, and such great projects as the Thames barrage, will tend to recreate the busy river scene of the eighteenth century. Under the south approach road are the bridge's great engines, original and perfect, a possible nucleus for a leisure enterprise.

71

The future of monuments

Above and left: tourists at Tower Bridge, the ever renewed raw material of our greatest future industry

Cities live by enterprise. In the late twentieth century, and in the next, we can be sure that Britain's role is unlikely to be an imperial one; the British will have to live on their wits. Britain already attracts a vast tourist trade, which can only grow. If a reasonable decency is to be maintained in tourist areas, it must be accepted that they too have an environmental capacity.

In short, it is necessary to create, or discover, new monuments to spread the load, to even out the pressures on Westminster Abbey and the Tower. These necessary treasures stand, ignored, all round us in the great heritage of Victorian and Edwardian buildings. The theoretical evaluation and appreciation of these buildings is now well under way, and the government has recently taken great steps to encourage preservation, and to prevent the careless greed that destroys one listed building of architectural importance *every* day.

Unfortunately, Ministerial admonitions are inevitably a little late, and are generally negative; a preservation order forbidding change.

Britain has a system which lists over 100,000 buildings as of historical importance, but relatively weak controls. Some countries have very powerful controls, but, as in France, over a mere 15,000 buildings. Others have hardly any. In the US even the award of a 'landmark' plaque is no safeguard against demolition by an owner who feels that the ultimate dollar may be escaping him.

It is therefore necessary, and urgent, that a more positive attitude towards our herd of white elephants is adopted. We must begin to see them for what they are: ASSETS. Assets in cities to stand against the serried curtain walls; assets which remind us of the continuity and meaning of city life; assets which provide an escape and a relief from the overwhelming coherence, the one-dimensionality, of our culture.

Assets, however, such as these depend on our attitude towards them. In the dark ages the Romans forgot their history; temples and arches disappeared. With their rediscovery and restoration they more than earn their keep today. Our new monuments need to be similarly discovered, to be publicized, and, above all, they must be allowed to survive until their value is accepted.

Death of a monument: Pennsylvania Station

Above: the statue of Cornelius Vanderbilt, founder of the New York Central Lines, at the foot of the south front of Grand Central Station
Left: Park Avenue with the north side of Pan Am building entirely dominating the original tower. McKim, Mead & White's Racquet Club building at right indicates the original scale of this explosively changed street

In the nineteenth century the railways carried the same emotional charge as does the aircraft in our own time. Everything happily yielded to this new technology, which with all its convenience, speed and safety, still inflicted terrible wounds on town and country. These wounds remain unhealed. The urge to bring the steam train into the heart of the city was universal, and nowhere more ruthless and ingenious than in New York. As in European cities, the railway stations were conceived as triumphal termini, the seal or crown of the transportation achievement. This pride produced, until quite recently, some of the greatest expenditure (and thus the most valuable and meaningful monuments) of our cultural history. Nineteenth-century architects brought to their work an immense industry, and a hard-won respect for the language of previous architecture. It was an age of measuring. Their sketchbooks were full of useful details from their cultural travels, which were worked up into immensely complex structures. Their confidence and their competence were immense, and from the great engineers they learned that all problems could be solved by industry and application.

The two great termini in New York are Grand Central, and the Pennsylvania station. Each is an example of the collapse of a great building in the face of change. Grand Central is one of the engineering wonders of the world: layers of railway tracks under Park Avenue terminating in splendid Roman halls. The great tower which marked the station effectively dominated the miles long stretch of Park Avenue and the stately hotels and apartments on either side.

After World War II the area, always fashionable, became a target for developers eager to turn the value of the street to their own ends. The first new building, Lever House, was also the first of the glass skyscrapers. It set a style that has conquered the world, a glass box on a two storey podium. Its relation to the neighbouring stone-faced cliffs was both churlish and inefficient, but the image of the glass tower, which had haunted modern architecture since the 'twenties, had become a reality.

Soon after, an infinitely more serious building was built diagonally across the street. Mies van der Rohe and Philip Johnson's Seagram Building fitted precisely the four storey blocks at its rear and made a memorable group with the brownstones at the side and McKim, Mead & White's Racquet Club opposite. For a few years a remarkable urban sensation existed, ordered serenity. However, it was not long before the pressure on the adjoining buildings grew intense and they and the whole street rapidly turned into a forest of glass blocks, indifferently reflecting each other. The Pan Am building, the largest work by Walter Gropius,

Death of a monument: Pennsylvania Station

Above: detail and left, general view of the south side of Grand Central Station

loomed over the Grand Central building and suddenly it wasn't there any more. And neither was Seagram. It was swallowed up in the maze.

The technical problems of threading the foundations of a building as large as Pan Am through four layers of railways tracks were immense; their triumphant resolution is an enormous feat of US technology. At the end of it all the building, though gigantic in scale and entirely humourless, is somehow a success, probably because the top is a landing pad for the airport helicopter service (a splendid example of multiple use). In place of the spires of the early skyscrapers (each was often an extraordinary architectural invention) the sight of the mechanical butterflies rising from the Pan Am building gives an equivalent sense of excitement and of participation in the twentieth century.

From the south side of Park Avenue, Pan Am is set well back behind the station entrance, and its sunlit façade always looks good. Pressure for air space is, however, so intense that another similar block was proposed to be built over the great waiting halls on the south side. Here the low building is at present dominated only by a splendid and elaborate sculptural group which symbolizes the railway terminal, and gives notice of the spectacular Roman interior. The vast halls in the rush hour (a truly terrifying spectacle) by their height and grandeur make bearable the intense press of humanity. The effect of physical pressure and tension which in the new Penn station turns one almost immediately to neurosis and hysteria, is here somehow released. The psychological effect of 'waste' space is nowhere more clearly demonstrated. These halls (and those of the old Penn station) are necessary healing elements in the competitive city.

The passing of Grand Central station* as a nineteenth-century monument is a loss, but at least it has been overlaid by buildings of an even wilder improbability and monumentality, and the net result is probably a gain.

---

* 'French in spirit, but with no evident prototypes, is the Grand Central station, New York, built in 1903-13 by Reed & Stem and Warren & Wetmore. More efficiently organized than the Pennsylvania Station, its concourse is one of the grandest spaces the early twentieth century ever enclosed'. Thus Henry-Russell Hitchcock in *Architecture nineteenth and twentieth centuries* Penguin Books 1958.
He notes that the 'organization of the tremendous complex was probably the work of Charles A. Reed (?-1911) and Allan H. Stem (1856-1931)', veteran railway architects. Whitney Warren (1864-1943) and Charles D. Wetmore (1866-1941) were probably responsible for the 'dignified and well scaled detailing'.

Death of a monument: Pennsylvania Station

Such is not the case of Pennsylvania station where a technically competent but architecturally callow structure has replaced McKim,

reduced to a bare minimum, with low, mean spaces and corridors to accommodate an awesome number of people. Above the squalor rises the usual office block and the new Madison Square Garden sports arena.

The ingredients of a wonderful building existed in the programme, a truly complex brief in both the technical and developmental sense. Yet nobody has risen to the occasion. By separating the arena from the office block the architects have simplified their problems. They have also reduced the meaning of the total complex. An age confident of its architectural language would have attempted an integration. It is precisely this failure, and the hundreds like it, that throw the whole problem of city redevelopment into question, and which reinforce the negative, protectionist argument. Hardly anyone wishes to preserve anything without good reason, but one can be almost certain under present conditions that a new building will be a bad building. The gradually stiffening controls over building all over the world are a part of a growing public reaction to the poor quality of modern commercial architecture.

Left: the new Pennsylvania Station, an entirely undistinguished office block
Below left: the main entrance, used by many thousands daily
Below: the office block with the new Madison Square Gardens arena at right

Death of a monument: Pennsylvania Station

Above left: McKim, Mead & White's design for Pennsylvania Station
Above: the general waiting room
Left: the restaurant
Following page: the concourse of the now demolished station

The partnership of McKim, Mead & White was the dominant force in American architecture from 1880 to world war I. Both McKim and White had been pupils of H. H. Richardson but they moved away from his ponderous Romanesque style to something more in keeping with the time, a period of remarkable wealth and growing sophistication. Their build-ings are not extraordinary when one comes across them, just very good in a matrix of building which is often of incredibly high standard. Their great contribution is that they profoundly influenced their contemporaries into a sober, Roman style, an achieve-ment (according to Sir Charles Reilly) to compare with the effect of Wren or Jones. Charles Follen McKim was born in 1847, Stanford White in 1853. W. R. Mead, the business partner, joined in 1880 and the firm grew vastly over the years to become the prototypical plan-factory (such as Skidmore, Owings and Merrill in our own time) that was essential for construction on the American scale.

Their buildings, once the great opera-tion was established, became in-evitably more mechanical, particularly after the death of the original de-signer partners, McKim in 1909 and White in 1906. The decline is said to date from the death of Joseph M. Wells, an associate of the firm, in 1891, whose Villard houses had set the firm on its academic career.

Their incredibly numerous works in-clude the University Club, the library at Columbia University, the Tiffany Building, Madison Square Church, Madison Square Gardens, National City Bank, the Morgan Library, Penn Station, all in New York.

Death of a monument: Pennsylvania Station

PENNSYLVANIA STATION 7TH AVE

Death of a monument: Pennsylvania Station

For centuries, central areas of cities have been the mainsprings of intellectual and social life. In prototypical US cities central areas are today run down and deserted, or else well advanced on the cycle of slum, followed by clearance, followed by commercial redevelopment or the new permanent slum of the low cost housing project. Within these miserable, minimum blocks there is no hope of growth, assimilation or change; no prospect but violence and alienation.

In this cycle the middle classes leave the city and do not return.

The source of city decay is richly complex. Its roots are in the very heart of our modes of perception, in the methods we have of measuring ourselves and in our idea of progress. In the worship of growth and productivity we have been unable to conceive ends, only means. We need more and more of everything, endlessly, and our industrial base and our living standards depend on it. The static, slowly evolving city of the past cannot stretch to accommodate the new dream of rapid and continuous expansion.

In the world of the developer, always piratical, the search for a higher productivity has brought an intense scrutiny into every aspect of building and in the process the architect has been largely eliminated. In central areas, buildings are readily calculated by estate agents' clerks and their values and specifications are pretty much the application of routine standards. Frills are never contemplated, thus unnecessary to eliminate. After all is settled, the architect is appointed to apply the module of his choice.

The concentration on ever higher returns, on stringent economies in all directions, results, without exception, in poor architecture. History is full of examples of mean streets and meagre buildings in which the life-style of the occupants can never be improved. Unfortunately our technology allows us to build meanly at an enormous scale, and to make huge profits in the process.

In such a cultural situation, monuments carry a subversive message, of conspicuous consumption, of lost erudition, of values beyond the mundane. They are reminders of our better selves, our communal responsibilities and of our present slavery to the requirements of the production process. It is no wonder that there is so much pressure to replace them with plastic packs for conveniently processed people.

Above: the only available view of Pennsylvania station. There is an extraordinary lack of documentation on this enormous and important building

Notes towards a general theory

It is true that throughout history architects have constantly returned to the simple geometrical shapes, cube, cylinder, sphere, pyramid for inspiration and as a kind of moral imperative. There is something of primal virtue in simplicity and certainly our eyes and minds are constructed to simplify and analyse into primary shapes and solids. We automatically 'correct' complex configurations into simple forms, and primary forms and colours seem to affect us deeply.

At the same time, the human mind has a tendency to elaborate, and to complicate, and it is perhaps no accident that simplicity is always characteristic of early phases of civilizations. The Egyptians built the pyramids at the beginning of their civilization, when the simple social structure allowed an equally simple formula to express it. Later periods in all civilizations tend to floridity and rich luxuriance. Late Roman architecture shares with the Baroque a feeling for complexity, for the grand scale, and it reflects, at the same time, a complex social background. It similarly expresses the contemporary requirements for new and varied building types, for which there was no precedent, or need, in earlier times.

When society changes, so does its architecture; the fanciful and luxuriant Gothic world died under the logic of double entry bookkeeping, and humanism brought architects back to the path of virtue, the elementary solids and noble simplicity. Yet within a hundred years it was all complexity again, and stayed so until the French Revolution and the concomitant austerities of the neo-classic revival.

In effect, the whole of architectural history can be seen as an alternation between ideals of elementary simplicity (virtue) beloved by the theorists and art historians, and periods of tangled complexity, which are always somehow more popular, and challenging, for the practitioners. Each periodic recall to virtue results in the neglect and decay of the buildings of the previous period. Roman temples provided useful columns for Christian churches; Gothic cathedrals caused embarrassment in the age of elegance. Victorian railway stations are equally embarrassing today.

It has taken three generations of architects and critics to establish the modern movement in architecture, and to do so required a fanaticism that determinedly ignored the past. This theoretical drive excused (and continues to excuse) vast areas of inadequate building on grounds of 'modernity' and 'simplicity'. We have quite simply destroyed the past, and our feelings of continuity with the past. No architect under fifty can even think of designing in any other style but 'modern'; none can speak in the dead languages of historical architecture, and very few can even understand what the buildings mean.

DESIGN FOR R.A.P.E. (Rectangular All Purpose Extension) FOR LONDON'S PUBLIC BUILDINGS

The recent controversy over the façade of the Tate Gallery illustrates the simplifying, reducing tendencies of our time. A vociferous public protest prevented this outrage

Above left: the existing front
Left: the proposals for the new extension
Above: an accurate and sarcastic comment by Garland in the Daily Telegraph

Notes towards a general theory

No generation of architects could have been so isolated from tradition since that of the early Renaissance. While their commitment was to the past, to stones that could be measured, ours is to a misty future. Our thinking is future oriented towards a world of mobility, of instant communications, of temporary, disposable structures, of continuous change and transition. We have to think in terms of vast population increases, of a building programme that must in thirty years build more than everything built in the world to date. We can be sure these buildings will be modern, clean and elementary, because that's the way accountants, and system builders, like it.

In this welter of new buildings, new things, and continual change, all cities will be submerged, and any regional differences ironed out. Already it is possible to travel the world and see only the foyers of Hilton Hotels, to view from your standard bedroom the elementary glass towers of Dallas, or Denver, or London, or Brussels.

In this new cityscape the fragments of the past that remain take on a haunting and poignant value. Even where an isolated church cowers in a canyon on Wall Street it asserts a human value, provides an architectural measure, and a social landmark. It provides the place with a recognizable identity. Even unremarkable buildings serve remarkably in this context, and deserve our love and care.

How much more valuable then are those great monuments of the immediate past that still litter our cities like stranded whales. A vast intelligence and ingenuity was expended on them; their complicated skylines still dominate our cities, though perhaps not for long, for they are mostly without protection.

We have been slow to recognize their tremendous values, in the changed situation of the future city. At present the buildings (such as the Foreign Office or Street's Law Courts in the Strand, London) appear to the inmates to be cramped and uncomfortable, mainly because they are crowded and overused. Their architectural value is obscured by careless maintenance, and by minor irritations on functional grounds. People have changed and the building has not.

In this situation there are many who would like a rapid replacement by something modern. But such a view would take no account of the building's true value, of its place in the city scene and the city's vitality, of its share of a city's invisible tourist earnings. The logical course is to examine the building, refurbish it, and provide the modern services, and to take the pressure off by providing alternative accommodation for the excess population.

Left: Wall Street, New York

89

The Pool of London. Note the effect of the new development, adjoining the Tower of London, on the grain of the city. Such forms have no capacity for growth and change

Notes towards a general theory

By this method the building can be preserved to play its more important role. In the future city we will need monuments, places to visit, to look and wonder at, for this is the purpose of our hard won mobility. In the coming years of mass international transportation, when whole populations will move each summer, the pressure on the older, established monuments will be unbelievable. Already the numbers are vast, and the pleasures of visiting are greatly reduced. This great surge of affluent, leisured visitors must be spread more evenly. Those monuments that now attract only a handful of enthusiasts will one day earn their keep as national treasures, if they can be preserved for a few years more from our short-sighted greed and carelessness.

In the 'twenties, at the beginning of the modern movement, our great men preached purity and simplicity, and forty years later the remaining pioneers are still trotted out by their commercial masters to display their elementary building blocks. In the meantime their simplistic philosophy has, by the magic of modern communications, been externalized in whole cities, and, enshrined in the hearts of bureaucrats all over the world, become an offical dogma. Particularly in planning theory and practice we find elementarism everywhere: single purpose areas (housing estates, factory estates), single purpose buildings (office blocks, apartment blocks), single purpose utilities (roads, pipelines, pylons), all following their own particular routes and dogmas divorced from the total community they are supposed to serve.

If we analyse buildings of before the theoretical watershed, we find their complexity of form supported by complexity of use, as well as a complexity of architectural and symbolic meaning. Buildings were usually combination buildings, containing and subsuming many different functions. Tower Bridge owes its form to its contradictory functions and is enriched by their resolution. In the same way we might be able to enrich our own buildings by re-thinking their programmes to provide a variety of accommodation. And, in fact, where this has occasionally been done an infintely more civilized building has emerged.*

---

* The German Rathaus or town hall always includes an excellent public restaurant. Early skyscrapers were not quite so concerned with prestige as at present. They always included shops at pavement level. The variety of subsequent food smells is one of the delights of New York.

Notes towards a general theory

Left: the Maltings, Snape, an old barn re-structured as an opera house and concert hall for Benjamin Britten by Philip Dowson of Arup Associates
Above: warehouses near New Quay, Liverpool, magnificent buildings in search of a new role.

In effect, complex requirements produce complex buildings. Ours is a society rapidly becoming more and more complicated, yet our buildings are largely impoverished, reflecting very little of our growing needs.

Because all urban tendencies are today towards a spread, suburban growth, we need to create antidotes. In itself, spread cities are not diseased, nor yet are they true cities. Suburbia is a mode like any other, and its social danger is that it separates out the family into an independent unit. Secure with built-in entertainment, the family feeds upon itself and loses social cohesion. The resultant problems of teenage delinquency, middle-aged boredom and old age loneliness are all too familiar to the middle classes, who have lived the suburban life for a generation or two.

These problems of affluence now begin to affect larger and larger numbers of people, and to reach classes singularly unprepared for a non-communal life. Once upon a time the introspective pleasures of life on one's own acre were sought by the educated few, as a distraction from city social life. Today it is almost compulsory for vast numbers of US citizens, whose cities have become too dangerous to live in.*

To create social cohesion requires a great social investment, but it must be done, and soon. To survive, a society, like a person, must grow in proportion; private life and public life are both essential. Our technology has tended to promote private life (the motor car, radio, television), at the expense of the public sector. (Galbraith's dictum 'private affluence and public squalor'.) We need more than we at present realize to build and run baths, theatres, concert halls, museums, art schools. These are the structures needed to balance the factories and housing estates, to create the nuclei around which new cities can grow.

If we look around we find that there are numbers of large, often beautiful buildings waiting for these uses. The best new theatre in London is a converted warehouse; an old engine shed has become a theatre in the round; a Suffolk barn has become an opera house. Warehouses, today of less and less value as distribution methods change, can convert to an infinite number of uses. In this way good buildings can be saved, and we can make necessary social investments in an economical and intelligent way, a way which also grows the invisible earnings of tourism and culture on which we will live in the next century.

---

* Saint Louis, Missouri, in 1969 has seen a murder a day; most big US cities do much better.

Plant a seed to grow a city

We can predict with some confidence, barring the holocaust, that our population and our productivity will rapidly increase. To take a short term view, in say fifteen years, the population of Britain, for example, will increase by five million ($9\frac{1}{2}$%) and productivity by at least 45%, and more likely nearer 80%. With this vast increase in scale (5·3 million people in new dwellings, plus all the necessary schools, shops, hospitals, etc.), we will find the problems of preservation becoming an ever smaller consideration. A mere 100,000 structures are listed as of architectural merit (though this ignores the vast areas of splendid, anonymous building which makes up the matrix of the mature city), and this is a fraction of a single year's production.

Much of the new building will inevitably go into new situations, new towns, expanded old ones, and into the outer regions of the great cities; literally, into the fields.

Once upon a time urban growth was set off by some physical or geographical incident — a river ford, a crossroad, a defendable pass, a sacred place. Today any stretch of productive farmland will do. Services are easily provided. All that is missing is a good reason to build it *there*.

Cities with a good reason grow faster and richer, but, more important, they stay alive beyond the impulse of their initial founding. They are capable of regenerating themselves, repairing their own tissue, through an internal economic and social dynamic.

This is hardly the case with our new towns, our expanded villages, those miles of suburbia tacked on to the already inadequate centres of the great cities. We have built, not cities, but housing estates, factory estates and very little else. These places are financed in the short term, and have the look and feel of temporary accommodation. The inhabitants hope to move on, to follow the economic treadmill that seems to require wage earners to live surrounded by others in the same bracket. In these circumstances the environmental quality can only diminish, as a visit to any older housing estate will show. Successful inhabitants move out; the unsuccessful stay put; the buildings become physically obsolete; the financing system places responsibility on a distant and increasingly bored bureaucracy. Finally it seems there is no alternative but to pull it down and rebuild, thus destroying the few remaining social strands that make the place bearable. In British practice this process should be repeated every forty years. In the USA, perhaps every twenty.

There can never have been a more wasteful mode of growing a town.

left: banners at Expo 67, Montreal

Plant a seed to grow a city

Yet to subvert the massive bureaucracy and the political dealing that is involved in building a new town is an impossible task. No planner could create an organic growth with every factor against him, with every one of his proposals either a tried and true failure or a risk impossible to contemplate in the circumstances. An impenetrable net of economic constraint, precedent and administrative complexity, hangs over all new city growth. It cannot be conquered.

But, perhaps, just once or twice, it might be outflanked.

To build a new city we need an occasion, a gesture, a meaning. We also need a massive injection of money, over·and above the provision of the minimum dwelling stock.

This money is needed to establish the place, to provide the focus and reason for the city; the seed money for its future self-regenerating growth.

Such necessary sums do not figure in the calculations of any country's Treasury. They produce no short term economic return, and thus have no apparent validity.

At least that is so in the case of investment in the apparatus of our daily lives. In other cases, where the accountants are technically at a loss, money is freely available: for aircraft unlikely to fly, for rockets which never leave the pad; for technologies which most scientific opinion considers to be of highly dubious value (such as the Concorde); for prestige in various departments.

The British spent £3 million on a pavilion at Montreal's Expo 67, and many other nations spent a good deal more. The benefits, if any, were intangible; yet the Treasury, in this area, accepts the necessity for expenditure, and acknowledges the value of the gesture in promoting our culture and way of life.

To bring this kind of promotional money into the field of environment would make spectacular changes, physically and spiritually. The easiest way might be to promote a world exhibition, to create the heart of a new city. Montreal invested £400 million to produce Expo 67 and at the end of the exhibition had lost £100 million. But the gains are outside this accounting. The city has been restructured: new motorways, a new underground railway, a vast upsurge in economic growth of every kind. The exhibition site itself, reclaimed from the St Lawrence river, is a massive gain. Built in less than three years, Expo 67 could feed, entertain and transport 500,000 visitors a day, the equivalent of the core of a city for three million.

Above: wind sculptures and the Gyrotron at Expo 67
Left: air view of the island reclaimed from the St Lawrence river

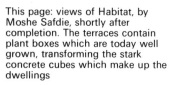

This page: views of Habitat, by
Moshe Safdie, shortly after
completion. The terraces contain
plant boxes which are today well
grown, transforming the stark
concrete cubes which make up the
dwellings

Opposite page, above: the US
pavilion at Expo 67, a geodesic
dome by Buckminster Fuller
Below: a collage of modern
monuments which could form the
nucleus of a city centre

Plant a seed to grow a city

It shows a sad lack of foresight that most of the pavilions have now disappeared. Such an investment in infrastructure, roads, services and transport could form the basis of a new city. The pavilions provided by the participating nations could have become very easily the cultural buildings for which new towns wait in vain. It only remains to add the suburbs. In the case of Montreal, Habitat demonstrated the most elegant and sophisticated housing concept in the world, the crystallization of many years of research and opinion from all over the world. There it will probably remain, an interesting demonstration. In a properly co-ordinated investment programme, it would simply keep on growing, recovering its development costs, creating the housing component of the city.

Most world exhibitions provide precisely what is most lacking in new towns; choice, variety and the competitive involvement of great talents — especially the latter. Cities, even new cities, require great buildings, as landmarks, elements of physical identity in a matrix of normality; they are elements of spiritual identity which create the necessary climate of social involvement. Great buildings help to produce great cities, fill citizens with pride, help to sub-sume private ambition within the collective, because they stand as symbols of the collective.

Marina City, Chicago, B. Goldberg and Associates

Post Office Tower, London, Ministry of Public Buildings and Works

U.S. Pavilion, Expo '67 Buckminster Fuller

Guggenheim Museum, New York. Frank Lloyd Wright

Notre Dame de Ronchamps, Le Corbusier

Habitat, Expo '67, Moshe Safdie

Parking

Parking

Parking

Services

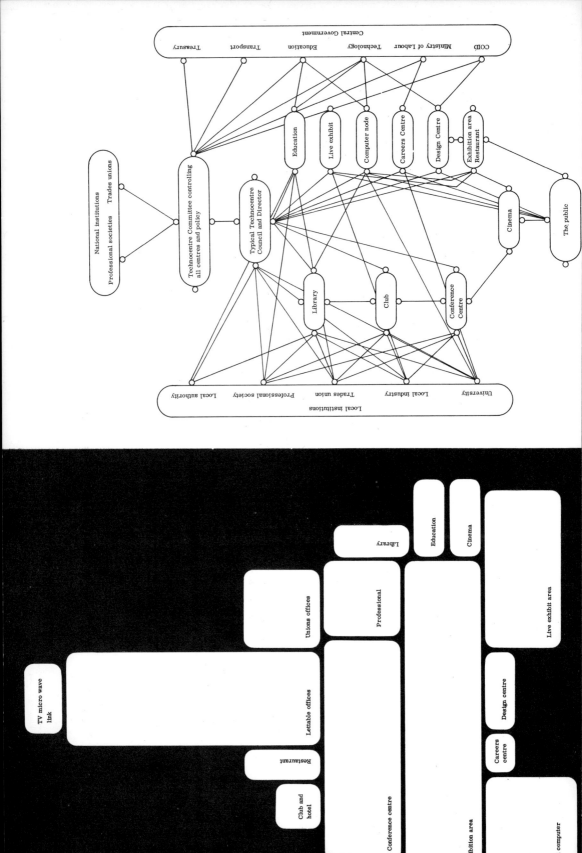

Plant a seed to grow a city

An exhibition is an opportunity to acquire a collection, a demonstration of the best available talent, a marvellous enrichment for daily life, and an investment in tomorrow's tourist trade.

Even if the possibilities of obtaining a major world exhibition are few, there are numbers of other lesser spectacles which might be used in a similar way: the Olympic games, purely national exhibitions and so on. At another level the establishment of a major technical facility produces a fall-out in value which can be capitalized to create a city, rather than a group of housing estates.

For example, a recent proposal by the Ministry of Technology to erect seven 'Technocentres' in Britain could provide a spectacular growth node for a new town or a way of reviving an old one. The technocentres are to consist of the headquarters of engineering professional associations and trades unions, a club, a conference centre linked to the other centres by television, an exhibition, computer centre, a restaurant, cinema and many other elements, all interconnected and each one more or less capable of paying its own way. A healthy subsidy for uneconomic elements was provided by an office building on top. Such a building is a good example of how a multi-use structure can be put together, to fulfil a social necessity, and actually make a profit. Its social role in a city could only encourage growth and raise values in its vicinity. As a centre-piece for a new town its effect would be to attract industry and to establish the elan so conspicuously absent in new development. It would be a monument.

In the end a city depends on its internal energy and self-confidence. The planners' role is to create the situation within which confidence is established and energies released. It is not a problem of negative controls, but of manipulating a vast number of complex interrelated factors, so that investments are made, in a sense, naturally, inevitably; that money is made, rather than saved; that social benefits accrue from private as well as public expenditure.

Above: diagrams of the elements and organization of the Technocentre concept

101

Questions of identity

Cities that are built or rebuilt within a very short time tend to monotony and repetition in their physical structure. This reflects also their social situation, for the inhabitants of newly built suburbs are usually remarkably homogeneous in their social and economic aspirations. This homogeneity tends to reinforce the original inhabitants' view of themselves, and confirms them in their life styles, prejudices, etc.

This is the case both for new towns and for new suburbs. The older suburbs tend to reflect the values of previous generations and thus are unsatisfactory backgrounds for the life styles of the second generation. The latter seldom feel called upon to defend the thoughts, or buildings of their fathers. This is the problem of the older, emptying, suburbs, and it is part of the larger problem of continuity, and of identity in our culture. With us the cult of the new is a force constantly reiterated by a formidable communications apparatus, which also spreads a cult of conformity.

In the face of continuous pressure to equalize income and opportunity, of being a consumer in a mass society whose choices are both limitless in theory and incredibly restricted in practice, the individual requires constant reassurance as to his unique identity. When religion ceases to offer general consolation or provide a way of communal life within which the individual is both subsumed and sublimated, we must search for alternative psychological supports.

One of the most common is role-playing: the selection of a suitable stereotype and adapting oneself to the inner and outer requirements of the role: hard business man; efficient, or helpless, housewife; tweedy professional; artist; jet setter and so on. The role, thus embodied, becomes the identity of the individual who as time goes by becomes incapable of any other role. It requires a major upheaval, or a war, to change one set of role-players into another set, and of course after the emergency is over the adjustment to a third role is often painful.

In terms of the built environment, or of objects generally, role-playing requires props of various kinds. The ownership of objects is the most important clue to individual identity, and sometimes the game is very subtle indeed. The cuff on a man's coat that actually unbuttons, or the cut of the waistcoat are clues from which one can identify a member of a class or an aspirant to a socially stratified life style.

Left: portrait of Sigismund Malatesta, Lord of Rimini, in the Tempio Malatestiano. This building, by Leon Battista Alberti, provided an irresistible impulse to architectural theory in the Renaissance

The relation to one's tailor is part of the whole range of identity building gambits which go under the general word patronage. To patronize someone is to buy or appropriate a part of their identity

Above: the Tempio Malatestiano, by L. B. Alberti

Left: London houses of about 1840, infinitely discreet and adaptable. The style was derived for middle-class living from the classical tradition re-established by Alberti and Palladio. Within such an integral matrix of building identity is created by subtlety of detail: a bay window, a painted door, a decorative fanlight or balcony railing

and thus reinforce your own. Sigismund Malatesta (1417-68), a minor North Italian war lord, has survived as an individual, and was admired as an intelligent and forceful man in his own time, almost entirely by his patronage of artists and architects. He literally built himself immortality.

In our own time the pressure for equality, and the dominance of evanescent cult figures, as well as the many alternative ways of spending money, have removed most of the temptations to do likewise. The whole cultural climate is organized to immortalize artists (for, as Andy Warhol says, about fifteen minutes) and not their patrons, and conspicuous consumption by the very rich only serves to make them the target of the communications machine.

The possibility of building one's own immortality in the Renaissance way is therefore no longer valid, and our identities must be reinforced in other ways.

The ownership of a work of art, however, if no longer guaranteeing survival after death, is at least a potent indication of one's taste and income level. Surrounding oneself with a collection provides also a constant intellectual stimulus and spiritual refreshment, an observation so true and banal that no one could possibly have written it down for at least a century. A collection is thus a way of establishing identity, and this applies equally to other personal or family objects: books, furniture, and above all the dwelling itself.

Most modern buildings are constructed for anonymous clients. That is, the spaces and surfaces are simple, bland and without personality. It is expected that the occupier will fill the rooms with his own vibrant persona. And, as few people have the talent for this sort of thing, most rooms remain bland, characterless, and are easily given up by their ungrateful owners. In fact, no one wants a room empty of character. The first impulse of the wealthy is to reach for an interior decorator.

An alternative is to commission or to search for a dwelling that in some way externalizes your own requirements for identity. Where you will feel 'at home'; a room, as Christopher Alexander says, with a memory. Such rooms, usually the product of alteration and adaptation, are to be found in old houses, which also carry powerful charges of identity-building imagery. The possession of a great house confers greatness, of an elegant house confers distinction; and it also creates for you a way of life which enables you to be your better self. Though social studies prove that the physical environment is low on the list of factors affecting people, above the middle income bracket it becomes constantly more important. This is the fastest-growing part of the population.

Questions of identity

In terms of the city, the analogy is very similar. We need to feel at home, but at our best. We need to be surrounded by buildings and objects of value, importance and beauty. Above all, they must be individual, idiosyncratic and preferably unique. The test of a city is its showing in the postcard business. Here the great cities of the modern world, with infinite wealth and productivity, do very badly compared to fifteenth-century Florence or Venice, which had only a fragment of the power and potential.

Identity in the city is only partly a question of scale. A good big monument is splendid, but much of the pleasure of cities comes from small scale invention and complexity: a doorway, a bay window, a spire, an element suddenly seen and exploited in the context of the street. These are fragments, the result of intelligent intervention or forethought, that provide the markers by which one remembers and creates a mental structure of a city. More than the height or size of the glass fronted office block, it is those fragments at street level, or on a skyline, that remain memorable. It is in just these parts that modern building is so helpless, and where buildings of an older tradition are so strong.

It is these elements which can be seized upon to bolster both a community and an individual identity. Old buildings carry over-tones of meaning, some now only very crudely recognizable to us. The architectural vocabulary was capable of many moods, grave and gay, through which we can still be touched. To recognize the language, and the players, to be able to see the jokes, is the richest pleasure of living in cities; to play the game is in itself a mode of establishing identity.

Above and left: Victorian building in London 1850-70

A flexible city building system, capable of sustaining a vast range of social levels and economic activities without disrupting the physical structure

Incremental growth provides a lively visual pattern within an accepted harmony of scale

Tentative conclusions

The magic of cities: romantic towers and gloomy chasms of New York; human contacts and associations that conceal much incidental squalor. These social interchanges, becoming outmoded by developments in technology and methods of distribution, need to be recognized and valued for their therapeutic properties. Shopping, once a daily necessity, now becomes a social pleasure, and requires suitable surroundings

In this discussion there can be no conclusions. We are truly in a state of rapid change in social and technical conditions; the very nature of our society is being transformed through a technology which is both liberating and oppressive. The disappearance of poverty and the prospect of the good life for all brings us squarely to the consideration of what the good life consists. Most of the products of the high culture of the past, the buildings, the paintings and sculptures, were intended for a tiny minority and they tend to be overwhelmed by large numbers of visitors. The same can be said of the countryside, the wild high places, the lonely beaches. They cannot and must not be denied the affluent masses, and they are easily destroyed by more intensive use.

The preservation of good things begins now to be more or less accepted as essential to our continued existence, but we have hardly begun to make enough good things for our own time; and we have been slow to realize how valuable and necessary is our inheritance. By making the gestures of commonality, our ancestors set up the markers of human progress. Unnecessary gestures, expensive and impractical. Yet these are the very objects we use our new found affluence to visit. If we are to civilize a mass society we must learn to spend, to live a little, to be as free with life as we are prodigal with death.

The greater part of the good life is freedom: to choose, to talk, to argue, to play and to work, and the widest choices and the best talk are found in cities. There is a magic in human association, in congregation, and in diversity. Only by contact and discussion with our peers do we reaffirm our humanity, discover our own thoughts. By argument and association we retain our dearly-bought liberties.

By their form cities promote or retard this growth of choices: their richness and variety are directly related to land values, access methods and architectural intention. For the visitor the city unfolds another magic; the magic of memory and association, of dreams revisited, the counterpoint of past and present. The romance of cities: New York from Brooklyn Bridge, the towers bloodied in the evening sun; the Thames at twilight, the bridges, the muddy shore and ebbing tide; the slowly waking lights, the spires and the great dome of St Paul; cities by night, lonely walks through echoing, haunted streets; in early morning, the buildings washed with gold. Everyone carries these images in his heart, images of power and complexity, and beside them our plans look thin and amateurish.

Why is it impossible to rebuild in the city without making a desert? Perhaps because we have not stated the problem correctly. We have been concerned only with logic and economy, virtues

Tentative conclusions

The small scale incremental growth of old cities provided an opportunity for a contribution by the individual owner or architect. Within a restricted street frontage all architectural problems can be resolved, and the restrictions themselves provide a stimulus to good design

Above: a thirteenth-century view of Florence
Left: Fenchurch Street, London

admirable in engineers and accountants, but hardly adequate as a base for a culture, or for the good life. A concern for the minimum produces nothing but the minimum.

In this book I have tried to put forward a logic of social need, and a more complex logic of individual and communal identity as a theoretical base for city design. A methodology founded on those premises would result in smaller scale development, based on actual need and not on purely speculative profit. It would avoid comprehensive development which does not allow the maximum of individual commitment and involvement. It would eschew the control of form by means of an arbitrary geometry, and use instead a system of clues derived from the existing environment: compatible heights, rhythms and fenestration. It would encourage the widest possible variety, and flexibility, of use, so that the activities concerned can grow and change without destroying the buildings.*

Such a system would allow a city to grow, but not to explode; a street to develop and change, but avoid excessive growth or decay; produce a consistent variety, and avoid a monotonous consistency.

Within this more complex logic there must be a place for the illogical, irrational object or building. We know little of the mechanisms of human behaviour, but there is in all of us a romantic love of the absurd, the unnecessary, the gilt on the gingerbread, which makes life not just bearable, but positively astonishing and marvellous, super-real.

Many remarkable buildings exist all round us, invisible under a shroud of grime and familiarity. Their rediscovery will give us both profit and pleasure, and their civilizing influence may help to counteract our present excesses. In the context of our cities even a third rate old building becomes a masterpiece when seen beside a modern commercial development.

We need those monuments, all of them, and many, many more.

---

* The experience with Georgian houses in London or brownstones in New York is especially instructive. They convert readily to flats, hotels, offices or studios without losing their original qualities, and often gain by the change.

Appendix 1
Tower Bridge: vital statistics

Above: detail of the opening span
Left: the works at Tower Bridge,
24th September, 1892

The bridge consists of two main towers, the river piers, and two smaller towers on the shore abutments, from which the suspension chains of the shore spans are supported. The opening span, with the two bascules pivoting at the face of the river piers, is 200 feet. The clear width of the shore spans is 270 feet. The bascules rise to a vertical position, leaving a clear 141 feet above high water level to the underside of the high level footways.

The headway of the shore spans is between 20 feet at the south abutment, and 23 feet at the north abutment and 27 feet at the river piers. The central span headway is 30 feet with the bridge down. The total length of the bridge is 940 feet; the approaches are 1,260 feet on the north side and 780 feet on the south side. The width between parapets is 60 feet, except across the opening span, where it is 49 feet.

Each of the river towers consists of four octagonal steel columns, 119 feet 6 inches high and 5 feet 9 inches across, braced by three sets of girders, from which the granite cladding is hung. The columns are elaborately stiffened and enlarged towards the bases, which are 14 feet between faces of the octagon, and rest on a granite bed 16 feet square and 3 feet thick. The bed consists of four stones, each 8 feet square, and this rests on engineering blue brickwork. The bases are hollow to contain the bridge machinery and are faced with finely cut granite.

Each tower contains two hydraulic lifts, capable of accommodating twenty-five passengers, as well as two flights of stairs. These lifts were for the pedestrians who would have to wait for the bridge to be lowered. One of the conditions imposed on the designers by the Thames Conservancy was that the bridge should be open for two hours at high water, so making this elaborate provision of lifts and high level walkways necessary. As the bridge opens and closes very efficiently in less than six minutes, they have never been used.

The high level ties, linking the two halves of the bridge together, are combined with the high level walkways and also carry the high pressure water pipes from the south pier to the north. The ties are rigid chains, made up of riveted steel plates 1 inch thick, and are connected over rockers on the main columns to the suspension chains to the shore towers. Since April 1961 the load on the ties has been transferred to 2 inch diameter lock coil steel cables suspended from the main top pins at the head of the shore span chains. The suspension chains in the bridge are rigid, girder-like structures, capable of acting in compression as well as tension, and stiffened to take up and distribute eccentric loadings.

The shore spans are hung from the suspension chains by 6 inch diameter rods at 18 foot centres, and consist of fifteen girders 3 feet 3 inches deep. Between these are longitudinal girders at 7 foot 6 inch intervals, supporting steel troughs $\frac{3}{8}$ inch thick and 6 inches deep, which in turn are covered with coke breeze lightweight concrete and wood blocks, now asphalted over. In the pavements are run water and gas mains and the hydraulic-pressure pipes.

From the shore towers anchor ties are taken deep in the abutments to girders bedded in concrete. The ties are box girders; they have a span of 80 feet and carry a tension of 1,000 tons.

Appendix 1

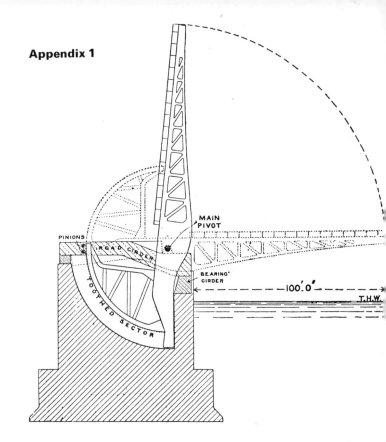

MAIN PIVOT

PINIONS

ROAD GIRDER

TOOTHED SECTOR

BEARING GIRDER

100'.0"

T.H.W.

Appendix 1

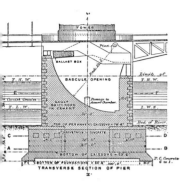

Above: a section through the pier showing the foundations, which are 26 feet below the river bed
Left: diagram of the bascules showing the principal dimensions
Below left: airview of the bascules in action
Below: engineering detail of the bascule chamber

The opening span is one of the mechanical marvels of the nineteenth century. Each bascule consists of four main girders projecting 100 feet over the water and extending 62 feet 6 inches back into the towers. They are 13 feet 6 inches apart, with transverse girders at 12 foot intervals; small transverse and longitudinal girders between these subdivide the floor into spaces 3 feet × 3 feet 6 inches, which are covered with domed floor plates $\frac{3}{8}$ inch thick. On this steel base are shaped timbers and a creosoted pine block road surface laid in asphalt.

The pivot for the span is 13 feet 3 inches inside the face of the pier, so that the underside of the soffit lines with the pier to provide the 200 foot clear opening. The rear ends of the girders rotate down within the bascule chamber. They are connected with transverse girders and loaded with some 365 tons of ballast, mostly lead.

The pivot itself is a shaft of forged steel, 21 inches diameter and 48 feet long, on roller bearings, supported by shaped fixed girders resting on the main tower walls. The total weight on the pivot is 1,070 tons.

The space between the opening leaves at the centre of the bridge varies between $\frac{3}{4}$ inch and $1\frac{3}{4}$ inches, according to temperature. When the bridge was asphalted it was discovered that it expanded rather more than the original calculation and it is now necessary to water the roadway on very hot days to shrink it to size.

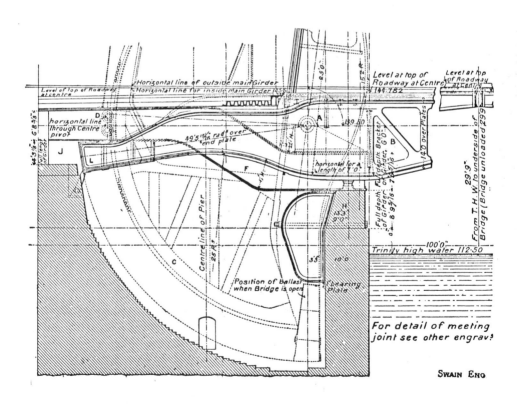

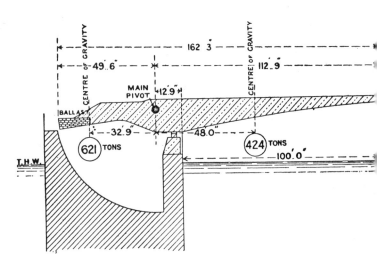

When the south leaf was tested it was found that with a full loading of 112 pounds per square foot the deflection at the end of the span was only $1\frac{3}{8}$ inches.

Because of the Board of Trade requirements, the engines and mechanical provision are generally excessive. The discussion at the Institution of Engineers, at the presentation of the bridge to the profession, was astonishingly free and acidulous on the subject. It was pointed out that hydraulic engines wear out very quickly; that the power required was only a fraction of that provided; and in any case the engines were of an old-fashioned type. The over-provision has, however, meant that the machinery is never under stress; adequate power is always available, and this has certainly been a considerable factor in the bridge's faultless performance for nearly seventy-five years.

The machine house for the boilers and engines is placed under the roadway on the Surrey side of the bridge. The steam engines pump water into four accumulators, one on each side of the main towers and a main accumulator in its own house on the south bank. An accumulator consists of a cylinder, containing a plunger, with a heavy weight on top. Water pumped into the cylinder raises the plunger, which then keeps the water under pressure of 700 pounds per square inch until it is required to move something. It is a simple system, but awesome at this scale.

Above and left: details of the hydraulic engines inside the river towers
Below left: diagram of the loads on the bascule
Below: diagram showing the principle of the accumulator, which provides the hydraulic power for the bridge

The hydraulic mains are remarkably flexible and versatile. Apart from the main functions of powering the bascules and lifts, the pressure is used for delivering water to the fire mains in the towers, and to the officers' quarters. The bascules are locked by hydraulic power, which also works the over run buffers deep within the bascule chambers, the signals and all the complex control and safety gear.

The tower accumulators consist of plungers 22 inches in diameter, with a stroke of 18 feet; the main accumulator tower houses two cylinders 20 inches in diameter with a stroke of 35 feet.

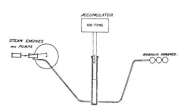

Within each river pier are two engine sets, one on either side, and each capable of driving the bascules. Each set contains two engines, a small one for normal opening and a large one for stormy weather. For very bad weather both together provide the power to raise the bridge against a wind pressure of 56 pounds per square foot.

The engines act on the bascules through gearing to rotate spur wheels on the toothed racks bolted to quadrants on the outside moving girders. The engines have three fixed single acting cylinders with plungers $8\frac{1}{2}$ inches in diameter and 27 inch stroke in the larger engine, and $7\frac{1}{2}$ inch diameter and 24 inch stroke in the smaller. The plungers work through exquisitely shaped connecting rods to crank shafts which revolve the gearing. There are a great many refinements and safety provisions: brakes, automatic stopping gear, hydraulic buffers for the counter balance, locking gear to secure the opening span in position, all worked by the ubiquitous hydraulic system.

Appendix 1

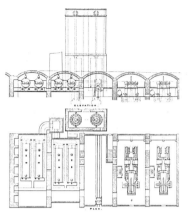

Above: plan and section through the south approach road showing the boilers, coal store and pumps, and the accumulators
Left: the Watt governor, the invention which prototyped the concept of feed-back by which a machine's performance can be automatically regulated, on one of the great steam engines.

Each bascule is normally raised by one engine, the other three being in gear and running idle, the water circulating through their cylinders and valves. Power can thus be varied, or the engine changed, or an engine brought into action at the opposite side of the pier.

Those water pipes which work the centre span locking bolts and other safety gear are necessarily exposed, and in the winter a mixture of glycerine and water, forming a small system of its own, is used to prevent freezing.

The hydraulic power for the bridge is generated in the arches under the south access road.

Here the two original engines are by Sir W. G. Armstrong & Co., Ltd, and are double tandem compound surface-condensing steam engines, each of 360 IPH, having high pressure cylinders $19\frac{3}{4}$ inches diameter, low pressure cylinders 37 inches diameter, force pumps $7\frac{3}{4}$ inches diameter and a stroke of 38 inches. One of these engines is enough, more than enough, to power the bridge. A third smaller engine was installed in 1958, which now relieves the two great engines. The latter are in perfect condition, beautifully painted and maintained, and should truly be one of the sights of London. Steam is supplied by four boilers 7 feet 6 inches in diameter and 30 feet long, producing a pressure of 85 pounds per square inch. Two boilers are generally in use, the others being kept in reserve.

The original coal supply system, with hydraulic cranes for unloading from barges and lifts is now unused, and coal is delivered by road. The result is untidy and the surroundings are anyway congested by motor vehicles. If the boilers could be converted to gas or oil, the whole area might be cleaned up and made accessible to the public. This idea is explored in the chapter on 'The social connection'.

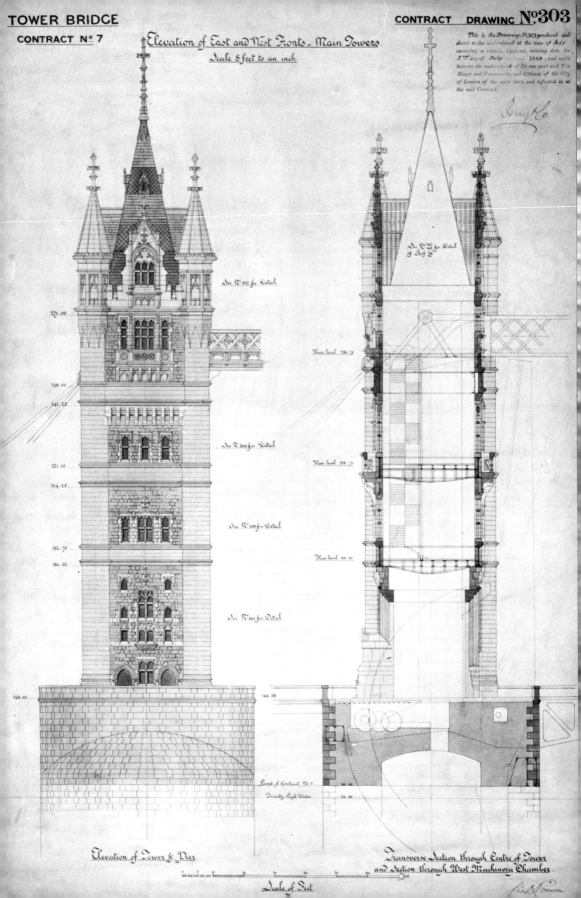

TOWER BRIDGE
CONTRACT Nº 7

Elevation of East and West Fronts - Main Towers
Scale 8 feet to an inch

CONTRACT DRAWING Nº 303

This is the Drawing Nº 303 produced and shewn to the undersigned at the time of his executing a certain Contract, bearing date the 2nd day of July 1889, and made between the undersigned of the one part and The Mayor and Commonalty and Citizens of the City of London of the other part, and referred to in the said Contract.

See Nº 312 for Detail

See Nº 309 for Detail

See Nº 308 for Detail

See Nº 305 for Detail

See Nº 308 for Detail

Floor level

Floor level

Floor level

Level of Contract Nº 1

Trinity High Water

Elevation of Tower & Pier

Transverse Section through Centre of Tower and Section through West Machinery Chamber.

Scale of Feet

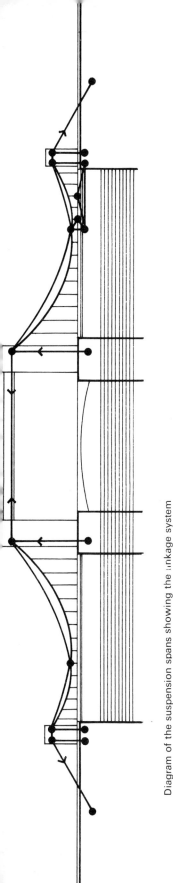

Diagram of the suspension spans showing the linkage system

Appendix 2
A structural appreciation by Edmund Happold

The structure of Tower Bridge is unusual. The bridge is a continuous one consisting of a pair of bascule leaves for the centre span, two suspension bridges for the shore spans, and two high level footways connecting the chains for the suspended spans over the centre. The main vertical features consist of two main towers on river piers and two smaller towers on shore abutments. The main towers are designed as vertical cantilevers from the piers. They consist of a skeleton of steelwork covered with a facing of stone. The opening span, between the two main towers, consists of two bascules pivoted near the faces of the piers like drawbridges, so that when they are raised ships can pass through the bridge. The bascules are counterbalanced within the tower piers, and the reactions caused by raising and lowering are taken directly to the riverbed through the piers.

Across the towers, from shore to shore, runs the tie system from which the shore spans are hung. This system is a series of rigid links, pinned at the joints and carried over the towers on rollers. The rigidity of the links varies; where the shore spans are carried from them on hangers the links are trussed to deal with unequal loading; where no weight is carried straight rods will do. The linkage system ensures that any settlement of the foundations of the piers would not affect the structure. It also means that the system is a mechanism and a load on one shore span could raise the other one. To reduce this movement an extra frame was inserted in the parapet on the Surrey side between the shore tower and the intersection of the two links.

The high level links extend from main tower to main tower and are hung from the top beams of the outer footway girders. The ends of these footway girders are cantilevers, tied back to the towers, with independent middle girders supported from their ends.

This design, a modification of that originally proposed by the City Architect, Sir Horace Jones, was carried out by Sir John Wolfe Barry. The Resident Engineer, Mr G. E. W. Cruttwell, presented a paper on the bridge to the Institution of Civil Engineers in 1896. Sir John was President of the Institution at the time and so took the chair. During the discussion which followed this paper several engineers cast doubts on the quality of the solution with a candour which would certainly cause deep offence if it happened today. The main question was whether there was justification for 'planting down in the middle of the fairway of the River Thames two impediments which bore such a large ratio to the total width of the stream'. Why could there not be a single span? Subsidiary questions were asked as to why a suspension system was required for the shore spans; could they not be lattice girders? Could a stiffening truss in the parapet have obviated the need for the stiffening linkage on the Surrey side? The biggest question of all was implied and answered several times, though never asked. Why have high level footways, which were never needed?

Sir John Wolfe Barry took the full opportunity of being chairman to answer his critics. He claimed that at the time of the initial design there was no gain in a single span as, in those days, there were two continuous lines of ships moored 100 feet from the centre line down the Thames, and the river traffic passed down the centre. Piers therefore caused no obstruction; three spans were more economic and also provided, in the piers, space for the lifting

Appendix 2

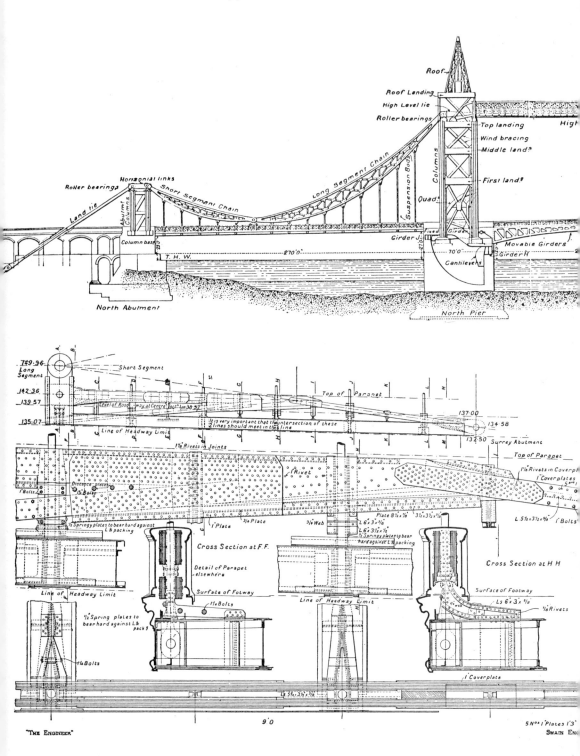

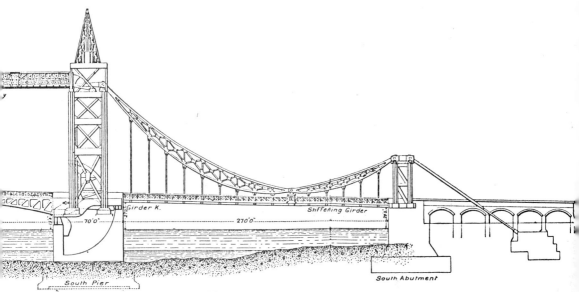

Top: a section showing the
arrangement of the steelwork
Above: the link in the suspension
span on the Surrey side
Left: detail of the stiffening
girder on the Surrey span

machinery for the bascules which would have been difficult to allow for in the bottom boom of a single span bridge. He also said that when they had carried out the design, the Thames Conservancy had very large powers as to the times of opening the bridge and had insisted that it would be necessary to keep the bridge open for ships for two hours at every high water. This requirement had never been enforced, largely due to the bridge machinery's ability to raise and lower the bridge in three to six minutes, but it led to the provision of two towers and high level walkways which, in turn, led to the adoption of the suspension principle for the side spans.

Here is probably the main criticism of the design. If machinery is put in to enable the bridge to be raised and lowered in under six minutes, why did the engineers go to the enormous expense of providing the tall towers and the high level footways? Not only that, but it led the designers, in trying to utilize the towers further, to offend engineering manners by mixing structural systems of cantilever bascules and suspended side spans. Good engineering design, like good architecture, has a literacy. Many structural systems can be chosen but they should never be mixed. Disorder results. Perhaps the designer fell into the same trap as many architects, that of having an emotional idea and insisting on building it, rather than evaluating alternatives and dispassionately selecting the optimum. Alternatively he fell into the trap many engineers do, that of not questioning the correctness of the limitations set on the design.

It is interesting to speculate what form the bridge would have taken if the footbridges had not been provided. Probably it would have been a swing bridge with double cantilevers turning on the piers. If so the machinery required would have been smaller and the piers correspondingly so. Certainly though it would have been less dominating and its monumental character, such a symbol to the world, have been lost.

Appendix 2

Criticism of the overall engineering concept should not be allowed to detract from the clarity of understanding of some of the detailing. For example, the main towers consist of a skeleton of steelwork covered with a facing of granite and Portland Stone, and backed with brickwork on the inside faces. There is a risk of bearing failure under the steel columns, which carry the whole weight of the towers together with the footways and part of the suspension chains and their loads. To obviate this risk, the designer provided layers of canvas and red lead between the granite pier and the base of the steelwork, in order to obtain a uniform bearing over the whole surface. To provide for expansion and contraction the columns were wrapped with oiled canvas to prevent the adhesion of the cement to the steelwork.

These columns were delivered in small pieces and erected by cranes on the piers. As load came on the columns there was a danger that the cross bracing would slacken and so the rivet holes at one end of the cross bracings were drilled sufficiently short of the corresponding holes in the columns to allow for any subsequent column contraction. The bracing ties were then heated by gas jets and, on expansion, riveted up. These induced stresses in the ties had been checked and subsequent loading only reduced them.

Certainly the designer was right to articulate the bridge. One of the piers of the then new London Bridge had subsided $1\frac{1}{2}$ inches when the load arrived on the foundations.

The scale of such a bridge was large for those days and the quality of detailing is perhaps best illustrated by how little trouble the bridge has given since its erection. The designer could have fallen into many traps. Certainly he felt responsible to the future. The collapse of the Tay Bridge had caused the Board of Trade to insist that bridges were designed for a wind load of 56 pounds per square foot. Sir John realized that the bascules provided a wind gauge larger than any before. By putting gauges in the machinery rooms they could record the amount and pressure of water used in each operation against all winds from whatever direction. He placed ordinary wind gauges on the high parts of the bridge. Experiments such as these, by many engineers, have led to the safe but economical wind design pressures of today.

Bibliography

Architectural history is well catered for in most libraries and a growing number of books deal with the increasingly respectable nineteenth century. Most of the earlier productions are apologetic, such as H.-R. Hitchcock's invaluable compendium, which searches for clues to validate the official history of modern architecture; others such as Robert Furneaux Jordan's *Victorian Architecture* find the subject thoroughly distasteful. Even a pioneering early work such as Kenneth Clark's *Gothic Revival* is somewhat lukewarm. In particular there is a chronic shortage of detailed study on such great men as Charles Garnier, Viollet-le-Duc, de Baudat, Guimard, Horta, Scott or Waterhouse, and the whole high Victorian period.

However, the point of this book is not to point to the academic fascination of a great era, but to explore the value of its monuments in the context of the present. Here there is even less guidance. Most current writing is simple complaint, or outrage at yet another cultural casualty. The most agonizing howl is Alison and Peter Smithson's dirge for the Euston Arch.

Sigfried Giedion *Space Time and Architecture* Oxford University Press, 1968; Harvard University Press 1954

Kenneth Clark *The Gothic Revival* 1928. Penguin books, Harmondsworth, 1962

Henry-Russell Hitchcock *Architecture Nineteenth and Twentieth Centuries* Penguin books, Harmondsworth, 1958. It includes a remarkably comprehensive bibliography.

Nikolaus Pevsner *Pioneers of Modern Design* 1936. Penguin books, Harmondsworth, 1960

Nikolaus Pevsner *Buildings of England* innumerable volumes since 1951. Penguin books, Harmondsworth

Pamela Ward, editor *Conservation and Development in Historic Towns and Cities,* Oriel, Newcastle upon Tyne, 1968

Lawrence Halprin *New York New York* HUD & NY Housing and Development Administration, 1968

The Regional Plan Association, New York, have published several valuable reports which bear indirectly on this study, and which explore the possibilities of development control in the context of the US economy.

Lewis Mumford *The Brown Decades* Constable, London, 1958; Dover, New York, 1955

Vincent J. Scully *The Shingle Style* Yale University Press, 1955

Reyner Banham *The Architecture of the Well-tempered Environment* Architectural Press, London, 1969. An attempt to find the history of modern architecture not in style but in nineteenth century technology.

Alison and Peter Smithson *The Euston Arch* Thames & Hudson, London, 1968

Giancarlo de Carlo *Urbino* Marsilio Editore, Padua, 1966. Study and intelligent plan for the Italian hill city

Colin Buchanan *Traffic in Towns* HMSO, London, 1963

Christopher Tunnard and Boris Pushkarev *Man-made America* Yale University Press, 1963

The editors of *Fortune: The Exploding Metropolis* Doubleday, New York, 1958.

Bibliography

William H. Whyte *The Last Landscape* Doubleday, New York, 1968. A critically important book on the effects of the move to suburbia and a basic text on how to control development.

Jane Jacobs *The Death and Life of Great American Cities* Cape, London, 1962; Random House, New York, 1961. The book that caused a radical change in attitudes to cities; essential to any understanding of city growth.

Jane Jacobs *The Economy of Cities* Random House, New York, 1969

Robert Venturi *Complexity and Contradiction in Architecture* W. H. Allen, London, 1968. Museum of Modern Art, New York, 1966. The first steps to a modern architectural theory beyond functionalism.

John Summerson *Heavenly Mansions* Cresset, London, 1949

John Kenneth Galbraith *The New Industrial State* Houghton Mifflin, Boston, 1967

Viscount Esher *York, a Study in Conservation* HMSO, London, 1968

Colin Buchanan and Partners *Bath, a Study in Conservation* HMSO, London, 1968

G. S. Burrows *Chichester, a Study in Conservation* HMSO, London, 1968

Donald Insall and Associates *Chester, a Study in Conservation* HMSO, London, 1968

Four reports to the Preservation Policy Group of the UK Ministry of Housing and Local Government explore every aspect of conservation problems, both architectural and economic, and suggest a variety of strategies and remedies for environmental improvement.

Acknowledgements

Edmund Happold, a partner in the firm Ove Arup and Partners, Engineers, of London, analysed the bridge at the author's request and provided the text for Appendix 2, including the basic diagram on page 121.

Technical information on Tower Bridge has been culled from the proceedings of the Institution of Civil Engineers, 10 November 1896, *The Tower Bridge: Superstructure* by George Edward Wilson Cruttwell, and the lecture given at Carpenters' Hall, London, by Sir John Wolfe Barry in 1893.

The drawings from these publications are reproduced by courtesy of the Librarians of the respective institutes.

The drawings on pages 26, 27, 28 and 29 are from the 6 volume publication *Le Nouvel Opéra de Paris, Tome I* by J. L. Charles Garnier reproduced by courtesy of the Librarian of the Royal Institute of British Architects.

The aerial views of Tower Bridge on pages 30, 90, 114 are by Aerofilms Ltd.

The engraving on page 32 is by C. C. Schramm, Leipzig 1735, the Anglesey Abbey Loan, Fitzwilliam Museum, Cambridge.

The architectural working drawings of Tower Bridge on pages 41, 42, 43, 44, 45 and 120 are reproduced by courtesy of the City Engineer, Corporation of London.

The photograph of St Katharine's Docks redevelopment on page 47 is by Sydney W. Newbery, courtesy Taylor Woodrow.

Photographs on pages 64, 65, 116, 117 and 118 of the Tower Bridge engines are by Jean-Louis Bloch-Laine.

Drawings of Pennsylvania Station are by courtesy of the Librarian of the Royal Institute of British Architects.

The photograph on page 84 is from the Radio Times Hulton Picture Library.

The photographs on page 86 are by courtesy of *The Times* and the Ministry of Public Buildings and Works.

Photographs on page 92 are by John Donat.

The photograph on page 93 is by Eric de Maré, © Gordon Fraser.

Photographs on pages 94 and 98 are by courtesy of the Quebec information office.

The illustration on page 99 is a collage for the *Sunday Times* by Crosby/Fletcher/Forbes. The concept of Technocentres was developed by a group consisting of Kingsley/Manton/Palmer, Crosby/Fletcher/Forbes and Dennis Lyons for the Ministry of Technology.

The painting reproduced on page 111 is *A Miracle of St Zenobius* by Domenico Veneziano (1410-1461) Fitzwilliam Museum.

All other photographs are by the author.